THE HEALING BOWL

THE HEALING BOWL

ANITA FISK

A HARLEY & FRIENDS ADVENTURE

ReadersMagnet, LLC

The Healing Bowl: A Harley & Friends Adventure
Copyright © 2019 by Anita Fisk

Published in the United States of America
ISBN Paperback: 978-1-950947-55-3
ISBN eBook: 978-1-950947-56-0

All rights reserved. No part of this publication may be reproduced, stored in a retrieval system or transmitted in any way by any means, electronic, mechanical, photocopy, recording or otherwise without the prior permission of the author except as provided by USA copyright law.

The opinions expressed by the author are not necessarily those of ReadersMagnet, LLC.

ReadersMagnet, LLC
10620 Treena Street, Suite 230 | San Diego, California, 92131 USA
1.619.354.2643 | www.readersmagnet.com

Book design copyright © 2019 by ReadersMagnet, LLC. All rights reserved.
Cover design by Ericka Walker
Interior design by Shemaryl Evans

This book of youthful adventure is dedicated to Noah and Graham, who epitomize wide-eyed wonder at every turn.

ACKNOWLEDGMENTS

THE AUTHOR WISHES TO acknowledge the literary contributions of mythologists Edith Hamilton, Robert Graves, and Thomas Bulfinch for their timeless stories that have captured the imagination of readers throughout the ages. In addition, a heartfelt thanks goes to Lisa B. Pontius, proofreader, editor, and typist, who challenges me to reach ever higher in my creative pursuits. Also, thanks to contributing artists Debby Zoback and "Ritchie Rich" Lopez for capturing on paper those images that lived deep inside my creative soul. Thanks to Shelly Nee and her creative team who provided serious technical support for this book. Most importantly, thank you to Noah and Graham Fisk whose antics and lively personalities have added a greater richness to the main characters of the Harley and Friends Adventure stories.

CONTENTS

Prologue 11

Part One: The Power of Friendship

Chapter 1: September 14
Chapter 2: Fuzzy Head 17
Chapter 3: Sammy 22
Chapter 4: Lessons 26
Chapter 5: "Football" 31
Chapter 6: Accident I 34
Chapter 7: Accident II 39
Chapter 8: The Stars 43
Chapter 9: Loyalty 47
Chapter 10: Blackbird 52
Chapter 11: Interpretation 56
Chapter 12: Heroes 61
Chapter 13: Time and Space 66
Chapter 14: Feathers 71

Part Two: The Quest

Chapter 15: The Crossing 76
Chapter 16: Arrival 81
Chapter 17: The Entrance 86
Chapter 18: Splitting Up 91

Chapter 19: Labyrinth 95
Chapter 20: Testing the Waters 99
Chapter 21: The Beast 104
Chapter 22: Water 109
Chapter 23: Tears.. 115
Chapter 24: An Offering 119
Chapter 25: "Hear Ye, Hear Ye" 124
Chapter 26: The Verdict 129
Chapter 27: The Harvest 134
Chapter 28: Touch of Earth.. 139
Chapter 29: Hygea.. 143
Chapter 30: Waiting 149
Chapter 31: The Gift 153
Chapter 32: Tears.. 157
Chapter 33: Close Call 162
Chapter 34: Brothers 166

Epilogue 171

PROLOGUE

On a rocky hillside a young goatherd leaned against his staff, gazing longingly across the vast Aegean Sea. In the distance he watched a flotilla of Grecian triremes. These spectacular fighting ships maneuvered expertly and strategically, rehearsing for superiority in their next naval battle. Such ships were a magnificent sight; to a twelve-year-old boy, they were the things of dreams.

The goatherd sighed deeply. His island home promised no more than fishing boats and an occasional cargo ship. The men inside those triremes were proof that another, more exciting world existed beyond his mundane life.

The oars of the triremes rose and fell with rhythmic perfection. The boy imagined himself among the 170 oarsmen, pulling his own blade through the crystalline waters. He could almost taste the salty brine on his lips. He could hear the winds groan as the warship buffeted the massive square sail. The boy knew that in a real battle, that sail would be down so that the ship could move at 14 knots… like a veritable water projectile. Those mariners were truly masters of the sea.

The bleating of his youngest charges drew him back. He had a job to do. His family depended on him to take the goats to pasture and return them by late afternoon to the makeshift pen next to the crude shack they made their home. The herd was the family's livelihood; his job was to remain vigilant.

Hungry predators sniffed around the perimeter of the herd, watching for the very old or the very young to slip beyond the watchful eye of their herder. One misstep in such rocky terrain could easily result in a twisted ankle, or worse yet, a broken leg. If the boy slipped, who would herd the goats?

He had to be careful. His mother often reminded him to get his head out of the clouds. He couldn't help himself. After all, he was more than just a goatherd. As often as possible, he relived the stories of gods and men that his grandfather shared over evening fires. That other world lay just beyond his reach. In time he would grab his part of that world.

For now, he could only dream.

PART ONE

The Power of Friendship

CHAPTER 1

SEPTEMBER

JFK MIDDLE SCHOOL TURNED out to be a pretty cool place—for a school. Having already survived sixth grade, Harley and his friends walked a little taller as they strode confidently through the maze of hallways. They were careful to avoid groups of eighth graders, but sixth graders, in all their innocence, were fair game.

Sixth graders stumbled around looking like deer in the headlights—scared to death and not sure which way to turn. After four weeks, many of them still lugged forty pounds of backpack. They had yet to figure out how to get from their lockers, to the bathroom or a drinking fountain, to their next class without being late. Four minutes between classes was not enough time for some of them.

Harley and his friends were seventh graders now. They had survived sixth grade chaos and could relax, knowing exactly the shortest route to every class. Harley felt older and wiser as he watched the parade of baby-faced packmules trudge through the halls.

Shaking his head, Harley said, "TJ, how long do you think before they figure it out?"

"'Bout the same as us," TJ replied, "nine or ten weeks." Then he laughed, remembering how stressed he had been.

Suddenly, two big boys, maybe 300 pounds between them, came barreling down the hall. Harley and TJ pulled back and flattened against the wall. Unfortunately, a couple of hunched-over sixth graders didn't move fast enough and were mowed over. One must have shrieked, because the two wrestlers stopped in their tracks and turned around.

"Did you say something to me?" spat one boy menacingly.

His buddy, pimple-faced and open-mouthed, leaned in closer and shouted, "My friend asked you a question! You got something to say?"

The terrified kid, trapped on his back with his arms and legs flailing in the air opened his mouth to speak, but uttered such gibberish that the two burly eighth graders broke out in uproarious guffaws.

"What a doofus," the pimple-faced boy roared.

"Let's get out of here," his buddy suggested, "before all this crying brings down Mr. Washington."

Just like that, they disappeared into the crowd… which simply stepped around the frightened sixth grader. It was a pitiful sight.

TJ strode over to the poor kid who simply couldn't right himself and offered him a hand. "Need some help?" The kid reached up, looking nervously over his shoulder. "Ignore them," TJ offered. "Wrestling team—they think everyone should be thrown down and pinned for the count."

"Thanks," the rescued sixth grader stammered as he scurried off down the halls, adjusting his heavy load.

"He'll be all right," Harley decided, as TJ rejoined him against the wall. Yep, Harley and TJ knew what it meant to be a true Eagle, the school's respected mascot. The seventh grade motto was "Lend a Helping Hand—Make a Friend," and that was just what TJ had done. "You're a good guy, TJ," Harley said, patting his friend on the back. "Before long that kid will be following you around like a puppy."

"Knock it off, Harley," TJ grumbled. "You're just jealous that I beat you to the punch."

Students at JFK earned eagle feathers for kind acts and good deeds. It was likely that sixth grader would report TJ to his homeroom teacher, who would tell the principal. Next thing, TJ's name would be added to the Celebration Wall. A kid with lots of feathers got privileges.

"This is going to be a good year," Harley smiled with satisfaction.

TJ watched the rattled sixth grade round a corner in one piece. The poor kid was so hunched over he looked like an old man. "Hope so," he added. "I don't want any surprises now that I know the ropes around here."

"I hear you," Harley agreed. "Me, too."

Chapter 2

Fuzzy Head

"It's got to be magic," TJ complained vehemently. "That's the only thing that makes sense."

"You're telling me that Ms. Clio is some kind of witch or something."

Harley slapped his own forehead. "And you think she cast some kind of spell on you." This time Harley let out a belly laugh that insulted his friend's dignity.

Even though Harley stood several inches taller than his best friend, TJ did not back down. "No, you jerk," he retorted angrily. "I… oh, I don't know what it is." He folded his arms and glared at Harley. "All I know for sure is that when class is over, I feel…" he paused to search for the right words, "I feel really funny."

Harley held back, though he was dying to shoot another barb at TJ. "What kind of funny? Like crack a joke—ha, ha, funny—or weirdo funny?"

"Just funny," explained TJ, "like my head is full and kinda fuzzy." He held up both hands, demonstrating a balloon-sized head being jostled in every direction. "It doesn't ever last very long, but I feel different than when I first get to class."

"You're a nut case, TJ," Harley teased; he couldn't help himself. "It's just another class like all the rest of them, and she's just another teacher."

"I'm not crazy," snapped TJ. "Just because you're older and bigger does not mean you know everything, Harley Delosian." TJ was almost in tears. He sniffed back loose, wet trails of snot that were threatening to inch their way over his top lip.

They walked the next block in silence. Harley knew he had crossed the line. TJ was the best kind of best friend any kid would ever want. Harley could tell him secrets because TJ would rather walk across hot coals than give up one of Harley's secrets. Last year, Harley's grandma had died. Harley had cried hard right in front of TJ, and TJ had told no one.

"Sorry, buddy," Harley apologized sincerely. "You're right! I'm a jerk, and there's lots of stuff I don't know."

"That's okay," accepted TJ. "It's just that something is going on, and I can't figure it out." Everything was right again between the friends—as it should always be.

"Hey, you guys," sounded high-pitched voices behind them. "Wait up!"

Two sprightly seventh grade girls in matching pink headbands rushed to catch up with the boys. They all lived in the same cul-de-sac and had walked together to and from school since they were in elementary school.

"Hey, Azlynn," Harley greeted the taller girl.

"Harley—TJ," Azlynn Kilpatrick responded. "How'd you guys do on that science test?" She rolled her eyes, indicating the absolute absurdity of it all. "It was the hardest test Mr. Brooks has given yet."

Tamiko Easter shuddered. "I studied for at least two hours last night." She frowned, kicking a loose pebble. "If I failed it, my dad's going to be really mad at me."

"You've never failed a test in your life, Tamiko," TJ reminded her.

As if she hadn't heard a word he said, Tamiko added, "He'll probably ground me, or worse, take away my phone."

"I reread the chapter and Mom quizzed me over my notes," TJ said. "I think I did okay."

"What about you, Harley?" Azlynn asked. "How do you think you did?"

"Well," he delayed. Harley knew better than to suggest he'd probably aced the test. After all, he spent hours last summer collecting cell specimens and drawing them in his notebook. "I think I did okay. You know that I like science the best of all my classes."

Tamiko, on the other hand, could diagram a sentence at the drop of a hat, and snag a direct object from across the room. She was a writer and had boxes of binders filled with short stories, poetry, essays, and several chapters of her pending novel. Harley and TJ could do none of those things.

Azlynn was a voracious reader. She devoured the entire Harry Potter series in less than a month. She was like the walking Hogwarts expert. It took TJ a whole quarter to get through *The Sorcerer's Stone*. Harley preferred comic books and anime.

The girls proved particularly helpful whenever Harley and TJ ran into problems with their English assignments. Even though the girls didn't necessarily depend on the boys to help them with *their* homework, they did spend a great deal of time together.

When they were little kids, they played for hours, reenacting some historical event that held TJ's attention at the time. Their backyards had been turned into the walk on the moon, the Battle of Little Big Horn, and the journey of Marco Polo. TJ explained everything, making sure the Samurai were not attacked with AK-47's. He knew history and how to bring it to life.

"You two trying out for basketball?" Azlynn asked. "Soccer season's over in a few weeks, you know…"

The boys looked at each other and offered noncommittal shrugs. "I don't know," they said at the same time.

"What!" Tamiko shrieked. "My dad says you gotta have a plan for everything." She had become rather obsessive about the order and organization of everything.

"I suppose you have your whole life planned," teased TJ, not really expecting an answer.

"Well, it just so happens that first I'm going to finish soccer, then I'm trying out for dance team, and then I'm going to start running for track…" she took a quick breath, "…then in the eighth grade, I'm going…"

"Stop!" shouted Harley. "We get it; your entire life is planned."

"Not really," Tamiko defended herself. "I don't know if I'm going to study medicine or if I'm going to law school." She looked squarely at her friends. "So there."

"We'll let you know as soon as we know about basketball," Harley signed, giving TJ a secret wink.

The foursome arrived at the center of the cul-de-sac. Even though they had had spats over the years, they always made up. It was great to have really good friends. They understood each other, but more importantly, they had each others' backs.

The girls turned towards their respective houses while Harley and TJ lingered at Harley's gate.

"Should I tell them about that thing?" Harley returned, closing the gate between them.

"You know what," TJ whispered, so as not to be overheard. "That funny feeling I've been getting in Clio's class."

"Oh," Harley remembered. "You mean that fuzzy head feeling at the end of class."

"Yeah, that thing."

"Maybe," Harley considered, "when the time's right."

TJ repeated, "When the time's right." He bumped his hip against the fence distractedly, pondering his dilemma. Azlynn and Tamiko were really smart, and TJ knew that they might know what was going on. If they didn't have an answer right away, they would tackle the "fuzzy head" phenomena until it was solved.

"Do you think they'll laugh at me or think I'm nuts, too?" TJ worried.

Just as Harley turned back to respond, a loud bang sounded from the side of his house. A flash of golden lightning rounded the corner and headed straight for him.

"'POLLO!" yelled Harley, trying to brace himself for the impending collision. It was too late. Apollo knew how to welcome home his boy. The dog launched his massive body with such momentum of adoration that Harley had no time to step aside. SLAM! The boy was down… another one for the canine.

Harley and Apollo rolled on the grass, laughing and whooping with joy. "You sure know how to make a kid feel wanted," Harley gasped, trying to catch his breath as Apollo tore himself away to nuzzle TJ at the fence.

"Hey, boy," cooed TJ, rubbing the nape of Apollo's fleshy neck. At this moment his world was right again… his best friend and best dog ever.

"TJ," interrupted Harley, "we've got practice in fifteen minutes. Meet you back here in five."

"Yeah, in five," echoed TJ. In the back of his mind, TJ repeated, "…when the time's right…" Time seemed to influence everything in his life. The silent march of time ticked ever forward in perfect cadence. Time was ephemeral; yet time could hold men hostage. TJ would wait until the time was right before he shared his secret with anyone else.

Chapter 3

Sammy

There were only a few practices left before the Divisional Tournament playoffs started on Saturday. The Strikers ad a reputations to uphold; they were the strongest, smartest ball-handlers in the Division. There was good reason the other teams worried; the Strikers played as seriously as they practiced.

"Come on, Harley," challenged TJ. "Let's get our laps done before Coach gets here."

"Harley, vroom, vroom," called another Striker from the track.

"Vroom, vroom," Harley called back. "Hey, Sammy, you ready for practice?"

"Sure am," the happy boy smiled hugely. "Hi, TJ."

"Hi, Sammy," TJ returned. "Did you already run your laps?"

"Sammy has one more lap to go," Sammy answered, moving between the boys.

"Run with us, Sammy," Harley said, slowing down the pace. The three ran shoulder to shoulder at a pace geared to Sammy's plodding gait.

Sammy was the team's greatest fan. He suited up faithfully for every match and cheered from his spot on the bench. Coach Kreller played Sammy every game, no matter the score or how crucial a win might be to the team's standing. He once told the team that each of them was a link in an unbreakable chain. "You hold this team together… each and every one of you." Coach had no favorites and no whipping boys; through his eyes they saw themselves as one—a single, powerful unit—a team.

As team captain, Harley yelled, "Strikers, link up for lines!"

Each athlete linked arms and ran to the goal line where they parted and assumed sprint position.

"Evens!" yelled Harley, who was in the odds group.

Every other boy shot off the line at full speed, including Sammy. As soon as the first group touched the line and turned back, Harley shouted, "Odds!" The boys pounded the ground heavily.

Each time they touched a line, they shouted, "STRIKERS! STRIKERS! STRIKERS!"

Before they finished their lines, Coach Kreller was on the field dumping out the net bag of soccer balls he kept in the trunk of his car. He watched the team warm up, pleased that they performed as intensely whether or not he was present. They were all fine boys and outstanding soccer players. For two seasons, he had trained these boys, setting high standards and consistency as their goals. He taught them strategies and to recognize opportunities to maneuver into the best positions to shoot, receive, and protect the ball. He was pleased at what they had accomplished thus far.

Harley made sure he ran the last line with Sammy. "Keep striking, Sammy," Harley encouraged.

"One more," Sammy huffed. "Keep striking!"

Sammy was a neat kid. Everyone welcomed the opportunity to look after him without him feeling like a fifth wheel. It hadn't always been this way.

After a few too many kids had been mean to Sammy and made him cry just because they could, Mrs. Crabtree came to school. They were in the third grade, old enough to understand.

"Class," announced the teacher, "this is Mrs. Crabtree and she's comes to talk with you about something very important." Sammy was not in school that day.

"Good morning, children," she began warmly. "Sammy's at home today, so I thought it would be a good time to share with you."

The students stopped rustling and looked to Mrs. Crabtree at the front of the room.

"You see, children, Sammy has a condition that makes him special. I'm sure you've noticed that he does things a bit differently, maybe a bit slower than all of you."

Two students giggled impolitely. Sammy's mother began walking slowly among the seated students. Standing next to the gigglers, Mrs. Crabtree continued, "He likes a good many things—the same as you. Do you play video games?"

Several students nodded. They even held contests to crown a champion for various competitive games. You bet—they loved video games.

"So does Sammy," she smiled, "and he loves many of the same things you like—rainbow slushies, Nerf wars, and, more than anything else—soccer." She paused, giving them time to connect. "Did you know that Sammy talks about you all the time."

Some students had worried looks. They were sure that Sammy was tattling on them for making him cry. One kid had held the bathroom door closed so that Sammy couldn't get out. Another had taken his dessert many times during lunch.

"He thinks of you as his best friends," Mrs. Crabtree stretched out her arms. "He tells me how nice you are and how he wants me to make something really special for you—his best friends."

Everyone was listening attentively. Even the kids whom everyone knew had teased Sammy and made him cry sat quietly—a little embarrassed knowing that the other kids knew they were guilty.

"Mrs. Crabtree?" a doe-eyed girl raised her hand.

"Yes, Audrie," Mrs. Crabtree said.

"Why does Sammy cry so much? I mean," she tried to explain, "he even cries when we read stories about animals in reading circle or when we watch a movie."

"You are so right," agreed Sammy's mom. "Sammy is a sensitive soul. He's especially tender about the pain of others. He cries because he wants to fix it so they don't hurt."

"Oh," Audrie said proudly, "That explains a lot. I cry, too, sometimes, but Sammy… well, you know."

"Yes, I do," Mrs. Crabtree said. "At your age you can sympathize with others, but you are able to control just how much sympathy you show. Sammy can't do that. He feels genuine sorrow and sadness, so he cries."

"We like Sammy," a red-haired boy shared from the back of the room.

"That's wonderful," Mrs. Crabtree grinned widely. "He likes you, too."

Ever since her visit to their third grade class, Sammy had become the center of every activity. No one ever again tormented him. When a new student arrived, he or she learned very quickly the unspoken affection and protection Sammy Crabtree generated in his classmates.

Every birthday in Sammy's class was celebrated with piles of homemade cookies. His mom was the best cookie baker in the world. Luckily for the Strikers, Mrs. Crabtree was team mom. On especially cold mornings, she served paper mugs of steaming hot chocolate topped with marshmallows.

"Okay, Harley," Coach ordered, "bring 'em in. I've got something to say before we begin practice."

"Strikers, circle up!" yelled Harley. "Hey, Sammy, bring it in. Coach has something to say."

"Bringing it in," Sammy repeated. "Bringing it in, Harley."

CHAPTER 4

Lessons

The seventh grade at JFK was sorted into four teams named for each homeroom teacher. Harley and his friends ended up together in Mrs. Sotomayor's team. She was their math teacher, and this year she supervised a student teacher, Mr. Vandercamp.

Harley and TJ joined the girls at the tables in the back of the room. Mr. Vandercamp reviewed their homework, checking to make sure they each understood yesterday's concept. In sixth grade, Harley and his friends had tested out of regular math into pre-algebra. Now they studied algebra, and they liked solving equations. Math made sense.

Mrs. Sotomayor was a master teacher who handled her classroom like the captain of a ship. She drilled conversion tables, probability formulas, and numerical operations including fractions and decimals. She was an expert at filling in the gaps so that her students were prepared to pass the exit exam into high school.

The room wasn't much bigger than their other classes, but the teachers ordered the potential chaos into efficient and effective learning centers. Everyone used soft, inside voices, as ordained by the master teacher.

"Mr. Crabtree," Sotomayor's voice rang out louder than usual. The entire room went silent. The question on everyone's mind, *"Was Sammy in trouble?"*

"Mr. Crabtree," she repeated firmly. "What must happen to the divisor when you are dividing fractions?"

No one breathed a sound.

Immediately Sammy jumped up to answer. "That's an easy one, Mrs. Sotomayor," he beamed. "You have to invert the numbers."

"Thank you, Mr. Crabtree, that is correct," she smiled her approval. "It appears that Mr. Crabtree paid attention yesterday. His homework bears witness. As for the rest of you…" her scolding voice faded into the background. Harley shot Sammy a thumbs-up sign of congratulations before returning to his own work.

The rest of the day went as well. In gym, TJ climbing the ceiling rope and rang the winner's bell. Though he appeared scrawny, his wiry muscles made him strong as a bull. Everyone cheered and patted TJ on the back. In Science, they constructed solar ovens, and in English they re-enacted "Paul Revere's Ride."

The students spilled out of the gym. Like a herd of stampeding buffalo, they raced for the last class of the day, Humanities I with Ms. Clio. TJ hesitated.

"You okay?" worried Harley.

"Sure, why wouldn't I be?" TJ snapped back.

"You've been having these fuzzy feelings again," Harley said.

"It doesn't hurt or anything. It just feels strange, that's all."

They were the last to arrive, just before the late bell rang. The boys shuffled along with the others to secure the warm-up vocabulary and a dictionary. They worked with a shoulder-partner to get the Key Word list completed in ten minutes.

Harley liked the way Ms. Clio ran her classroom. He knew exactly what to do; also, she was the best storyteller ever. They had finished exploring the cultures of the Indus Valley and had moved on to cultures surrounding the Aegean Sea, the Hellenes or Greeks.

Ms. Clio taught them about how cultures evolved, and how these ancient civilizations sustained their history through telling stories, art, dance, and religion. Harley really liked this class. He thought that TJ would be at home with all the history Ms. Clio shared.

He glanced across the room where TJ sat with his partner. A powerful sunbeam blurred the details of TJ's face, but to Harley he seemed okay. Harley had begun to pay closer attention to this friend's odd behavior in Ms. Clio's class. TJ hadn't said much more about his "fuzzy head," so Harley didn't bring it up again. However, he still worried.

"You finished?" Azlynn interrupted. "I've got mine done."

Harley looked back. "Almost."

"Hurry up! She's ready to start," Azlynn warned.

Ms. Clio rose from her computer desk where she took roll and recorded homework grades. She tugged down a huge wall map showing the geography of the Mediterranean Sea.

"We began here," she pointed, "generally known as… Tamiko Easter?"

"The Fertile Crescent," Tamiko responded quickly.

"Today the modern land of Iraq," continued Ms. Clio. "Remembering that civilizations begin in areas abundant in water and fertile land," she slid her hand southwest, "we find ourselves at the crossroads of Asia and Europe.

Byzantium straddles both sides of this imaginary road. It was later named Constantinople, and is now Istanbul in present day Turkey. The Black Sea is to the north and the Aegean Sea to the south." She turned to face the class.

The entire class listened and followed Ms. Clio's pointer moving rapidly to various key geographical locations on the map. This was a required class, and she was a serious teacher. As eighth graders, the students would get to choose either Humanities II or World History I.

"Today you will produce individual, detailed maps of the area as it was in ancient times. Your completed maps must be neat and colorful. Include the Caucasus Mountains on the northeastern border of the Black Sea, Troy, and the many large and small islands in the Aegean, Adriatic, and Mediterranean Seas. Here is a list of towns and geographical landmarks of Greece, Italy, and Egypt."

Tamiko, who sat closest to the front of the room, reached for the blank maps to distribute them at the head of each row.

"Use your desk maps and these two wall maps to help you locate every name on this list," Ms. Clio said, holding up a long list of names.

A trio of whispering students dared to ignore the teacher moving down the aisle toward them.

"You will have only this class period to complete the assignment," Ms. Clio said sternly. "Without exception." She stopped at the desk of one of the talkers. "I will accept no excuse for a sloppy or incomplete map."

She leaned over into the trio and whispered menacingly, "Stay on task or suffer the consequences. I do not want to hear any more about how hot the new kid is." She paused to stare each student into silence. "Am I understood here?" She ignored the titters behind her.

The next 45 minutes flew by. Harley had checked out TJ again. His friend acknowledged him with a look that said, "I'm fine."

"That's it," Ms. Clio announced. "It's time to clean up and turn your assignment in to the correction basket."

Like an army of ants knowing with precision their individual task, all tools and resources were stored in their proper places. The class returned to their seats and waited for Ms. Clio's closing comments.

"Tonight on the PBS channel they will be featuring a documentary that follows the myth of Hercules. I'd like it very much if you could find time to watch it and come prepared to discuss his trials and tribulations."

As expected, a few hands flew into the air. "Before you ask," she turned to her desk grabbing a stack of papers, "I have some light reading for those of you who are unable to watch the documentary. Pick one up on the way out."

The final bell blasted like a foghorn. Their school day was finally over. A gaggle of girls moved toward their lockers. Harley and TJ hoisted their backpacks and turned down the hall toward the exit doors.

"Did you finish your map?" Harley asked.

"I did," TJ returned. "You?"

"Yep," Harley said. "Did you know that there was an island called Delos, like my name even?"

"Kind of like the tip of the fingernail on the island Andros and the southern tip of Euboea…"

"Okay, that's too much," Harley stopped TJ's geography lesson. "I just wonder if my ancestors came from Delos—that's all."

Shrugging his shoulders, TJ mumbled, "Oh, I don't know… could be. Anyway, let's get moving. We've got an important practice today." TJ did know about Delos. It was the birthplace of Apollo and Artemis, but he thought it better to save that little nugget until later.

Leto, an abandoned consort of Zeus and heavy with child, could find no land to welcome her. Delos was rocky and barren. The wind and the water tormented this island until Leto set foot on its shores. Four pillars rose from the ocean floor to secure the little floating island. Here, Leto gave birth to twins. Henceforth, Delos rose from the most shunned, ill-fated island to the status of "heaven-built isle" of the gods.

Chapter 5

"Football"

Harley Delosian and Thomas Jarrell Harris, TJ, had been best friends forever. Tamiko Easter's family moved into the cul-de-sac before she started preschool. All of her brothers and sisters had attended JFK, leaving her some big, impressive shoes to fill. Azlynn Rose was the middle child of the Fitzpatrick clan. They had moved to the cul-de-sac a couple of years ago. Harley, TJ, and Tamiko liked her immediately.

As Harley and TJ neared their homes, they both noticed the motorcycle parked in the Delosian driveway.

"You got company," TJ said. "Remember we got to get to practice in a few."

"Okay," Harley said, slowing his pace.

The motorcycle belonged to Uncle Jim, his mother's older brother. In the same way that Coach Kreller loved soccer, Uncle Jim loved football. Jim laughed at the very idea of soccer being called "foot ball."

"Soccer—that's some kind of sissy sport," he insisted one evening over dinner. "You should be playing a man's game—American football, not this silly roll the ball around the grass kind of game."

"Jim," reprimanded Harley's mom, "leave the boy alone. He likes soccer and he's really good at it."

Uncle Jim, trying to play surrogate father to Harley, harrumphed loudly. "Girls play this game. Don't they?" he looked to Harley who had nothing to say. "Well, there you are, Val; it's a sissy sport."

It had become obvious to Harley that Uncle Jim had never in his life played 80 minutes of soccer. The game was intense, fast-paced, and grueling. More than that, it was a game of strategy and teamwork. Uncle Jim and his friends liked football because it was hard-hitting—a body slamming kind of sport.

Soccer, on the other hand, was a game of finesse. The less contact he made with other players, the more efficient his play. In football the quarterback had to read the defense before executing a play, after which the action reset. In soccer, every player had to read the entire field throughout the entire match, with the only real pause in action coming at the half.

"Uncle Jim," Harley interjected, "why don't you come to one of my games?" Uncle Jim had yet to show.

His uncle picked up his buttery corn on the cob and quickly began gnawing on the kernels. It was obvious to Harley that he was finished with the discussion of soccer versus football. The image of Coach Kreller popped into his head. Coach lived and breathed soccer. Harley respected that about his coach.

Some time ago, Harley learned that his coach had played college soccer. Many of the other coaches were volunteers and could hardly run down the field without huffing and puffing. Not Coach Kreller—he was lean and fit. If he ordered the team to do five laps or 20 crunches, he'd do them as well. The great thing about Coach was that he'd finish before anyone on the team. However, Harley was getting stronger and faster. He was up to challenging Coach Kreller's athleticism. By next season, he might beat Coach's time.

Harley smiled at Uncle Jim who was spooning more savory gravy onto his mashed potatoes. His mother winked at her son, suggesting that they shared an important understanding.

"Remember, boys," Coach would begin his pregame mantra, "a team is only as strong as its weakest player." He'd always pause at this point in his speech. "And," he would say, "every player is responsible for the success and failure of every other player on the team."

The boys would look at each other, nodding in agreement. They would hand slap each other both high and low. They felt special.

"That's what makes us a real team," Coach said, beaming. "Who are you?"

Excited and anxious to play, the boys would begin shouting in unison, "We are Strikers… we read the field… we strike the ball… and we always shoot to win!"

"Shoot to win," Sammy Crabtree would repeat.

"That's right, Sammy," Coach would always agree. "We shoot to win."

In Harley's mind Coach was the epitome of what a coach should be. All the boys on the Strikers respected Coach Kreller and none of them ever wanted to fall short and disappoint this man. In the beginning, Coach never once yelled at them, blaming them for a loss. He would sit them down and explain to them what had led to the loss. The tone of his voice encouraged them to want to learn, to better their skills, and they did. Now, they were the champions that other teams dreamed of bringing down.

The only team out there even close to defeating the Strikers were the Bombers, named for the military airbase at the edge of town. Harley knew that this team was good, but in his heart of hearts, he believed in the Strikers and he believed in Coach Kreller.

Chapter 6

Accident I

After dinner, Harley took Apollo to the doggie park to check out the latest doggie news. Apollo romped with glee... chasing butterflies, tennis balls, and doggie playmates. It was always the best time of the day.

Golden retrievers were great dogs and loyal companions. Apollo came to live with the Delosians the same year Trooper Charlie Delosian was struck and fatally injured by a drunk driver. That was almost five years ago, when Harley was just seven.

Trooper Delosian had pulled over a car with a broken taillight. It had been raining off and on all evening. Delosian had followed protocol when stopping a vehicle on a busy freeway. The driver, a young mother with babies properly strapped in their carseats, was more than cooperative. She was glad that this highway patrolman had brought the potentially dangerous situation to her attention.

"I have precious cargo in here with me," she told him, as the two cherubic toddlers jabbered happily. "If anything were to happen to them..." she trailed off, imagining the worst-case scenario.

"Consider this a warning," he smiled. "I am a parent, too, and I know exactly how you feel." He leaned in to make a silly face at the babies. They welcomed his funny face with giggles and cooing sounds. The trooper stood back up and said before turning around, "You take care now and get that light fixed as soon as possible."

Oncoming headlights immediately blinded him. A vehicle was bearing down on him at a dangerously high rate of speed. There was not enough time for the driver to brake or for the trooper to get out of the way. The last thing Trooper Charlie Delosian heard was the horrible screeching of brakes and a woman screaming.

Several hours later, there was a knock on Valoria Delosian's door. "Val," said the trooper who was Charlie's best friend, "there's been a horrible accident. Life in the Delosian home would be changed forever.

Harley was too young to understand the full ramification of what had happened. All he knew was that Daddy had gone to Heaven to help God. Whenever his mother was too sad to play with him, Harley turned to his puppy, Apollo, who seemed to love and understand him. Harley loved his dog more and more. They became inseparable.

Even now, at bedtime, Apollo would lounge at the foot of Harley's bed to get his well-deserved belly rub. Harley would tell Apollo his memories of his daddy that he couldn't share with his mom.

Holding a framed photograph of Trooper Charlie Delosian, a spirited little boy, and an adorable yellow puppy, Harley would begin with, "This is Daddy, this is me, and that's you." Apollo would paw Harley as if he understood. This went on for a long time, until Mommy came back to them, ready to pay attention to them and play again.

Now, TJ was a big part of Harley's best friend circle. It was Saturday, the first day of Divisional eliminations. Sixteen teams played in their division. After this weekend, only eight teams would remain. Single elimination was tough. Many players were seen crying after their team lost.

Harley did everything Coach Kreller had told the team to do. "I want you to eat a healthy dinner, prepare your gear, and go to bed early." After brushing dirt clods from his cleats, Harley laid out his red and white jersey. He packed his shinguards, his clean towel, a newly polished ball, and an empty water bottle into his sports bag. Now he could get a good night's sleep. On this night, Harley reviewed every play out loud. Apollo listened faithfully.

"Mom," Harley called bright and early, "I gotta go; TJ's waiting."

"Harley," Valoria yelled down the hallway, "not without a good-luck kiss." She crushed him into a well-intentioned bearhug. "Love you, son," she smiled, planting a maternal peck on his forehead. "I'll be there before the first pass."

By the time warm-ups were completed, families had filled the sidelines with folding chairs and picnic blankets. The Husky fans were dressed in grey and white, while the Striker backers were in red and white. Sammy distributed the practice balls to his teammates. They practiced a three-man weave, then ran the give-and-go. Balls were dribbled up and down the warm-up field. Harley understood that these were muscle memory as well as strategy exercises. It was important for players to react automatically to every situation during the match without having to think about what to do.

When balls rolled beyond the touchlines, Sammy would retrieve them and carefully practice his throw-ins.

"Way to go, Sammy," cheered TJ, "both feet on the ground!"

"Both feet," Sammy parroted happily.

Mrs. Crabtree and Mrs. Delosian always sat together. It was late autumn, the air was brisk but not too cold. The mothers sipped mugs of steamy hot chocolate while watching their boys warm up. Next to Mrs. Delosian sat an empty lawn chair. Some of the other moms thought it was in honor of Harley's father; Harley's friends thought it was for the absent Uncle Jim. Valoria never explained the empty seat; it just sate there. One thing was a constant—Apollo. Though he didn't really need it, Valoria always attached a leash to his collar while he watched. Soccer was in everyone's blood.

It was game time. The Strikers and the Huskies formed two lines facing each other at midfield for equipment check. The procedures were routine, but this match was the beginning of playoff season. Not only the players, but their families and friends along the perimeter knew just how important this game was.

The tension ratcheted up a notch when the referee beckoned both teams' captains to the center spot. He delivered his usual speech about safe play and exercising good sportsmanship. The captains were expected to repeat these instructions to their respective teams.

Harley knew all too well that Coach Kreller took these instructions to heart. He expected his players to be respectful and attentive in every practice and match. Anyone who goofed off or threw a fit was sidelined indefinitely. None of the Strikers ever made that mistake twice.

Each team moved into position. TJ's wildly printed purple and black goalkeeper jersey replaced his Striker red and white. He swayed side to side on the balls of his feet in eager anticipation. "Come on," he growled in a low, but threatening tone, "try me." He stared at the backs of his teammates. He knew how to read their every move. "I'm ready."

Harley stood tall in the Strikers' front line. He glances left, then right. The forwards were poised to advance. He checked over his shoulders to see that the midfielders and defenders were in place. Everyone was focused. Finally, he glanced back to his keeper. TJ gave him a thumbs up.

The referee blew his whistle and then dropped the soccer ball in front of Harley. He nudged the ball to his left. Parker Madison flicked the ball back to Harley as the frontline dispersed across the field. The Husky defense came to life and began their rush toward the ball.

Grey #14 moved into position to challenge Harley for possession of the ball. Harley was too fast and too sure-footed to lose possession. Easily, he dribbled the ball around the Husky before launching ten yards out to his right wing. Striker #10 nimbly zigzagged his way toward the goal. Maintaining their strategic distances from each other, the Strikers moved in unison downfield with him.

Striker #10 passed to #21, who in turn sent the ball to Harley. Staying even with the defender ten yards out until the ball left #21's foot, Harley faked and then took a quick dribble for a clear shot. A quick punch with his left foot sent the ball flying across the green, not into the net, but a perfect cross to #8, Josh Mancebo, who deftly deflected the pass into the goal. Lucas Herrera, #10, was the first to jump on him with a congratulatory whoop of delight.

The match lead went back and forth. The crowds on both sides of the field cheered with enthusiasm each time the ball changed direction. Even Apollo barked wildly every time Harley dribbled the ball past him. Coach Kreller never yelled out names when giving his players directions. Instead, he'd yell out jersey numbers, telling #10 that #8 was open, for example.

Every time a player was in position to head the ball, Coach would yell, "Sight it… Keep your eyes open!" At practice, Coach taught his boys to open their eyes so that they could watch the ball come their forehead. "Never lose sight of the ball… Never close your eyes… Use your whole body to redirect the ball's momentum."

The Striker fans began chanting, "SHOOT! SHOOT!" Then wham! Harley headed the ball over the Huskies and into the corner of the net. Near pandemonium broke out on the Strikers' sideline. Mrs. Crabtree grabbed Mrs. Delosian; both were jumping up and down wildly.

The referee blew the whistle, indicating halftime. Each team moved to its respective bench for a ten-minute break. Several moms helped Mrs. Crabtree pass out orange slices and bottled water to each player. Coach Kreller sat the team in a tight semi-circle.

"Great teamwork, fellas," Coach began, "but the match isn't over yet. You have set a rigorous pace, but look at them." He pointed to the Huskies.

"They are keeping up with you. You've got to step it up."

He was right and every Striker knew it.

"Crabtree," yelled Coach, "warm up. You're going in as sweeper."

Sammy usually played on the right on defense, but he had practiced the center spot as well. It was time for him to show what he had learned. He stretched his arms and shoulders. Then he leaned forward and backward, making sure his back was loose. Finally, he ran in place with high knees pumping. "Okay, Coach," he said. "I'm ready."

"Keep your eyes open, Crabtree," Coach Kreller reminded him. "Don't let those Huskies get through your defense."

"Eyes open, Coach," Sammy repeated. "Eyes open."

Chapter 7

Accident II

Sammy played the backfield right in front of TJ. Every time the Huskies offense came close to the goal, TJ would call to Sammy to sweep the area. "Sweep both sides, Sammy." Next, TJ would remind Sammy to roll the ball back to him. They had practiced the maneuver a hundred times.

The Huskies kept breaking through. "Stop those shots, keeper!" Coach called to TJ. He was on it. татTJ watched their passing pattern. It was predictable. Both TJ and Sammy were pumped.

The Striker defenders spread like a protective shield ready to mix it up with the Husky forwards. Striker defender #7, Buddy Duval, raced toward the offensive player who was encroaching on TJ. He stepped left - then right.

He circled the ballhandler so quickly that the Husky was unable to pass the ball. Instead, he sent the ball soaring toward the goal and Sammy. Both players tracked its trajectory. Sammy had to get into position to deflect the soccer ball.

He began stepping backwards with quick, short steps. He kept his eyes on the ball. "It's yours, Sammy!" shouted TJ. The shot was high. Sammy would have to head it. He knew how to do this. He had practiced and practiced. He stopped. His body tensed, bracing for the impact.

On the Strikers' sideline, Coach Kreller kept repeating, "Keep your eyes open, Sammy; watch the ball. Keep your eyes open, Sammy."

The ball dropped like a bombshell from the sky. Sammy watched it race toward his face. "Keep my eyes open," he reminded himself. The ball was only a few feet from impact. Sammy closed his eyes. In that instant he also lost his balance and fell backward—hard. His head bounced off the ground.

The soccer ball, too, hit the ground. TJ was on it in a second. Sammy lay flat on his back; he wasn't moving. "Coach!" yelled TJ as loud as he could, soccer ball tucked neatly against his body. "Sammy's down. He's hurt!"

The entire field went silent.

The referee whistled play stoppage, and all the players took a knee as Coach Kreller raced to where Sammy lay. Mrs. Crabtree held her breath. Mrs. Delosian grabbed her hand to comfort her. "I don't understand," Mrs. Crabtree cried, "he didn't even touch the ball with his head."

The EMT on the Huskies' sideline ran onto the field where Coach knelt next to Sammy. TJ kept the curious players at a distance. He knew that Sammy was in trouble. Coach waved in Mrs. Crabtree. The situation was grave, and the minutes while Sammy lay motionless ticked by like hours. An ambulance siren grew louder as it flashing lights cleared the roadway to the field. Sammy still had neither moved nor opened his eyes. Within minutes of its arrival, the ambulance whisked Sammy and Mrs. Crabtree away.

Fifteen minutes later the game was over. Neither team had scored another goal. The Strikers won the match 4 to 2. However, no one felt like celebrating. They were all worried about Sammy. Coach told them that Sammy must have hit his head pretty hard on the ground. He might have a concussion.

Monday morning at school was the worst day ever. The Strikers and their parents had spent the entire weekend at the hospital supporting Mrs. Crabtree. When the crowd of concerned friends grew too large, filling every vacant chair in the hospital, the doctor finally ordered them to go home.

"Sammy remains unconscious," he told them, "and his mother is exhausted." He looked at Harley and TJ, who had become fixtures in the waiting room. "Boys, there's nothing you can do for him right now."

"Can we come back tomorrow?" TJ begged, "after school?"

"Okay," the doctor gave in, "but only one of you each day, and you can sit with Sammy's mother in Sammy's room."

The boys looked at each other and then at their teammates. "One of us will be here every day until Sammy wakes up. Right, Strikers?"

"Right, Harley," they responded. "Every day."

"That's fine," said the doctor. "For now, go home and get some rest yourselves."

In every class that Sammy shared with a Striker, his desk was conspicuously empty. The students would look to the desk and then to the soccer players. Many offered sympathetic words: "I'm sorry about Sammy…I hope he will get well soon…We miss him."

In the hallway between classes, TJ turned to Harley and asked, "Do you think he'll be all right?"

"It's hard to say, TJ," Harley replied. "Nobody can know…except maybe God."

"But Sammy doesn't go to church," TJ reminded his friend. "You know that. Maybe God doesn't know Sammy's hurt."

They walked to their next class in silence.

Harley finally responded to TJ's concern. "God knows. Father Murphy says God knows everything."

Still worried, TJ asked, "But does it matter if Sammy didn't… you know…believe in Him the way we do on Sundays?" TJ stopped Harley from going through the classroom door. "Harley, will God forget about him in the hospital?"

"I don't think so," Harley said convincingly. "We're not going to forget him. That's for sure."

For the first time all day, TJ smiled, "Ain't that the truth."

"I'm going to sit with Mrs. Crabtree today," Harley said.

The somber group filed into Ms. Clio's class. She, too, had been at the soccer match and had witnessed the accident. Ms. Clio made eye contact with every student who stepped through the door. She waited until everyone was seated before speaking to the class. There was no empty chair in her room because Sammy didn't take Humanities I. However, every teacher on the seventh grade team knew Sammy Crabtree very well.

"It's quite obvious and most reasonable that Samuel Crabtree's accident has had a tremendous impact on you—on all of us. We must marshal strength on his behalf and share our strength with his mother. Sammy is in the hands of modern medicine, and according to the ancient Greeks, if his stars align, he should come back to us soon."

Tamiko Easter raised her hand. "Excuse me, Ms. Clio, but what do you mean about the stars?"

Chapter 8

The Stars

Using Tamiko's question as the perfect segué, Ms. Clio began the day's lesson. She moved to the wall map and placed the pointer on the Aegean Sea. "In ancient times people depended on the stars to guide them on their journeys. They determined that the stars aligned themselves in different patterns throughout the year—thus, seasons were born. They even tied their newly discovered star tracking to their everyday lives.

"That make sense that they looked to the heavens for answers," TJ observed. "I mean, especially the sailors who depended on the stars to show them the way home."

"Well, we still look up there," Azlynn added. "Different people look for God or Allah or even Zeus like the Greeks. Don't we?"

Another student jumped into the conversation, "Yeah, well, in the end they're nothing but balls of burning gas that don't even exist by the time we see their lights."

"You are correct," Ms. Clio explained. "There are two points of view about the heavens. Remember, however, that ancient man did not know the science that you do. Either way, the study of the stars has held man's fascination since the beginning of time."

Ms. Clio moved gracefully to the Smartboard and activated the internet. Several frames of the night sky appeared across the board.

"Release your imaginations and tell me what you see." She pointed to a cluster of stars.

"I count seven stars," Tamiko announced.

"Yes," Ms. Clio agreed. "The Chinese saw them as seven palaces of Shou Lao and the Hindi saw the seven Rishi or sages," she went on. "The Sumerians saw a heavenly wagon called the 'Charles Wain' that drove across Europe. To them *Charles* was the great conqueror Charlemagne. They weren't the only ones who saw a wagon. The Norse people called those stars 'Odin's Wain.'"

"Wow," observed another student. "All those people were looking at the same stars, but saw something different and named them something different."

"Yes, they did," Ms. Clio validated. "Even the Celtic people associated these same stars with the legendary King Arthur. *Arth*, or *Bear*, is part of Arthur's name. His full name means 'luminous bear.'"

Enthralled with the lesson, the students were studying the frames of night skies. Suddenly, Harley called out, "I know those stars," he pointed. "That's the Big Dipper." He sat up a little taller. "My mom showed it to me when I was a little kid. There's the handle that sticks out from a bowl…a dipper."

"Yes, Harley," Ms. Clio commented. "In North America it is called the Big Dipper, or more astronomically correct, Ursa Major or the Big Bear."

The teacher went on to explain how some Native American tribes saw the four stars of the cup as the bear and the three stars in the handle as the hunters. Then she added, "During the hunt, the bear would be injured and bleed. His blood turned the autumn leaves red, year after year."

The class easily connected to this concept. "The blood also fell on the robin's chest, staining it red as well." The room buzzed with interest. The teacher was ready to bring them full circle back to the ancient Greeks.

"In Greek mythology," Ms. Clio began, "the legend of the sky bear is an intriguing story." There was no storyteller as good as Ms. Clio.

"Tell us the story," begged the class. "Please!"

As was the way of the great Zeus, a beautiful maiden caught his attention, and he wanted to get to know her. She was called Callisto. Zeus successfully hid her from his very jealous wife Hera…or so he thought. When Callisto gave birth to a boy who would be part man and part god, she called him Arras.

It didn't take long for Hera to find out about Zeus's son. She was determined to punish Callisto by turning her into a bear and Arras into a hunter.

"Oh, no," cried Tamiko. "I don't think I like where this story is going."

Across the room, Harley could see that TJ was lost in his own thoughts. He couldn't help but wonder if that fuzzy feeling was inside his head again. Ms. Clio continued with the myth.

Eventually, the hunter and the bear found each other in the woods. Callisto recognized her son and tried desperately to speak to him. All Arras heard was the menacing growl of a bear. He notched his arrow and stood ready to defend himself.

"Waaaah!" the end of day bell sounded.

No one in class moved. "Please, Ms. Clio, finish the story," begged several students.

Zeus intervened. He would not allow a son to kill his own mother—even if she were a bear. Instead, Zeus turned his son Arras into a little bear and cast both mother and son into the celestial sky: Ursa Major and her baby, Ursa Minor.

"…Big Bear and Little Bear that you know as the Big and Little Dippers," Ms. Clio finished. She had their full attention. "Tomorrow we will continue with the Seven Sisters—The Pleiades."

The room emptied slowly as students talked about Callisto and Arras. Harley stood by the door waiting for TJ.

"Thomas," called Ms. Clio, "Thomas, it's time to go."

"I know, Ms. Clio," TJ answered. "…I saw them."

"Saw whom, Thomas?"

"I saw the mother bear and her son, the hunter, in the woods." He reflected on his experience. "He was really scared and he didn't want to shoot the bear."

"I know, Thomas," Ms. Clio tried to soothe his worry. "Arras really was a good son. Perhaps that's why Zeus chose to save him."

"Do you think Zeus knows that Sammy is a good son and might save him, too?"

"Why of course he would," she answered him softly. "What makes you ask?"

"Sammy needs help," he said. "I'm going to ask Zeus to help him." TJ picked up his backpack and slowly walked away.

"He believes," Ms. Clio whispered.

Sammy Crabtree lay in a deep sleep with his Ursa Major, his mother, tending to him, praying for him to wake up and be well again.

CHAPTER 4

Loyalty

"Back to Olympus again, my cousin," teased Phoebus Apollo in all his golden glory. "Have you given up on your mortal quest?"

"Don't you believe it," the daughter of Zeus and Mnemosyne snapped back. "I think I have found the first believer." She raised her hand in the air between them and waved a window into the future before him. "Look at them," she said with pride, "they actually care about each other." She showed the children at the hospital bedside of an unconscious boy of a similar age. "Those children are genuine and kind."

"That's not the point," Apollo reminded her. "You promised to find ten mortals who truly believe in our world."

"I know what I promised," she acknowledged. "My time has not yet expired. Don't give up on them so soon."

"My daughter," the mighty Zeus greeted her, "the beautiful and wise Muse of History, Clio, have you yet inspired them to value our influence and embrace our presence?"

"No, Father," she spoke quietly, "but I am closer. Almighty Zeus, Ruler of the Universe, shook his head in disappointment."

"You see those grains?" he reminded her, pointing at a gigantic hourglass. "They stop for no man and no god…they will not slow for you."

"I understand, Father," she bowed respectfully, "you are most kind and generous. I will not disappoint you."

Zeus promised her that he would bestow upon the mortals who occupied the land a longer and more prosperous life. He said he would open the heavenly vaults and shower mankind with Olympian generosity. Since the beginning of her quest, Clio was unable to discover one mortal who believed…that is, until now. However, she chose not to name the mortal until she could be sure.

"Why do you bother?" Apollo asked his big-hearted cousin. "They destroy each other in war in the name of religion and power. They cheat each other in both the pocket and the heart. Worst of all," he went on, "they disrespect the elders whose lives have given them opportunity."

"There you are," Clio said. "Are they not like us? Do we not become savages in wars against differences? Are there not those among us who have taken that which was not given? Yes, we give honor to Zeus and his brothers, but we do so not only out of respect, but also out of fear."

She reminded him that in the great battle of the Titans, Zeus had killed his own father, who had earlier destroyed *his* father.

"That mortal boy who sleeps," Apollo recalled, "Father Zeus could cure him as he can cure all of the suffering of mankind. However, he, as of yet, does not deem them worthy. And you want to change that." Apollo laughed, "Good luck, cousin." He then vanished into the broad sky.

Clio thought, "They have one trait that supercedes all others—loyalty." Clio recognized the honor in the kind of loyalty they showed toward each other. "They are good people," she called after Apollo. "You shall see for yourself."

From a large cumulus cloud a voice rang out, "Loyalty is honorable, but bravery is what defines a man. Give me a brave man first—then I will find his loyalty."

"Harley," asked Tamiko on their way home, "do you think he's awake yet?"

"I can't imagine sleeping for days on end," added Azlynn.

"He's not asleep," corrected TJ. "The doctor said he's in a coma." TJ recalled the horrible scene when Sammy's head literally bounced off the ground.

"I saw it plainly," Harley shared. "When Sammy closed his eyes and continued to stumble backwards, I yelled at him, trying to stop him." Growing up, Harley and TJ had hit their heads against hard surfaces many times. Neither of them had sustained a concussion. With Sammy, it was different. It was like a perfect storm of two powerful forces coming together. Harley thought he'd felt a tremble beneath his feet at the exact moment when Sammy and the earth came together…crashed against each other.

"My mom thinks that Sammy may have bruised his right temporal lobe," Tamiko told them. "That's probably what caused his concussion."

They walked the rest of the way, saying very little to each other. A pall of sadness followed them everywhere. Despite the vibrantly colored walls and the smiling animal faces that greeted visitors on the pediatric floor of the hospital, Harley's heart remained heavy as he approached the nurses' station.

"Excuse me," he said, trying to catch the attention of a physically imposing nurse in bright scrubs, one he hadn't seen before.

She looked up from her charts. "Yes," she began officiously, "can I help you?" Her nametag read, "Ursula Fisher, RN."

My name is Harley Delosian and I'm here to see Sammy…I mean Samuel Crabtree.

"Well, Mr. Delosian," Nurse Fisher continued, "Mr. Crabtree is unable to receive visitors at this time."

Harley's shoulders sagged in disappointment. "Um," he tried to explain, "Dr. Ammon said that one friend could visit with Sammy and his mother each day after school." He cleared his throat. "Today is my turn."

"So, you've spoken with Dr. Ammon," Nurse Fisher said. "Let me speak with Mrs. Crabtree. "She stood—all six feet of her. "I'll be right back." A few minutes later, she waved Harley down the hall.

Harley felt relieved. He padded silently toward Sammy's room. Harley didn't know what to expect. He remembered how his mother had reacted to his father's death, but Sammy was still alive. It was possible, though, that Mrs. Crabtree might be lost in her own world.

A cadre of cheerful bluebirds guided Harley to Sammy's room. Nurse Fisher eyed him carefully before she would allow his to enter. "Mrs. Crabtree needs a break. You offer to sit with Samuel so that she can stretch her legs. Do you understand?"

"Yes, Nurse Fisher," said Harley. He knew exactly what the nurse was telling him. Watching your unconscious child hour after hour can be emotionally exhausting. Harley could be alone with Sammy for her sake and for the sake of his friend.

"Good," Ursula Fisher said. She stepped aside so that Harley could enter the hospital room.

"Harley," whispered Mrs. Crabtree. She had dark crescents under her eyes. Though she smiled at Harley, her voice was laden with worry. "It's so good to see you." She brushed the hair from Sammy's forehead. "Sammy would be pleased if he were awake." A tear slipped down her cheek.

"Hi, Mrs. Crabtree," Harley said softly, "I want to be here. Everyone misses Sammy." Harley turned toward the sleeping boy. He seemed—Harley couldn't quite put his finger on it—like he was okay…he had a kind of smile in the corners of his mouth.

"He hasn't moved," Mrs. Crabtree shared. "He hasn't talked or opened his eyes. The doctors can't explain it." She clutched his chubby, boyish hands to her chest. "He's all I have, Harley."

Harley patted her on the shoulder. "Mrs. Crabtree, why don't you take a little break, I'll sit here with Sammy. I even brought a book to read to him." He pulled out a Marvel comic. "Sammy likes this guy. Anyway, TJ and the others are in the waiting room. I'm sure they'd like to hear all about Sammy from you."

"You're right, Harley," she said, standing and stretching. "I will take a short break." As she opened the door, she said, "Just talk to him, Harley; he knows your voice."

Nervously, Harley pulled up a chair closer to Sammy's bedside. He gazed at his innocent friend. "Darn it, Sammy, you should've kept your eyes open." He felt guilty scolding his friend. "I'm sorry, Sammy, I'm just so sorry that you got hurt."

Harley blamed himself for Sammy's accident. *If I had been a better captain—if I had worked more with you—if—if.* Harley could beat himself up with recriminations, with a long list of "If I had…" However, he came here to comfort Sammy, not lay out his own shortcomings.

He wiped his tear-dripping nose on his sleeve. "I brought Spiderman to read to you." He reached for his comic book, opened it to page one, and began reading with wonderful vocal inflections for each character. Harley was so engrossed in the story that he didn't see that a change had come over Sammy's face.

Sammy wrinkled his nose. His eyelids twitched as if he were struggling to lift them open. Without warning, Sammy reached out and grabbed his friend's hand. Harley jumped back, knocking over the chair. "What the heck," he yelled. "You're awake!"

Harley dashed into the hall. "Nurse Fisher! Mrs. Crabtree!" he yelled in scared delight, "he's awake! Sammy opened his eyes!"

CHAPTER 10

BLACKBIRD

Harley and Mrs. Crabtree rushed to Sammy's bedside. Nurse Fisher phoned Dr. Ammon. Sammy's eyes were wide open, but he seemed not to see them.

"Epimend," he called out in a raspy voice, "wait for me."

"Sammy," cooed his mother, "Mommy is here with you. Look at me, Sammy." A river of tears cascaded down her cheeks. Her baby was awake.

"Sammy," asked Harley, "who is Epimend?"

"I'm coming," Sammy called cheerfully. "I see the blackbird. I'll catch you, Korvus. Run faster, friend, I'm right behind you!" Sammy shouted. "You won't get away from me, crow!"

Nurse Fisher entered the room. "The doctor is on his way." She saw that Sammy's eyes were, indeed, open, and that he was talking. He seemed to be reaching out for something.

"I almost got it," Sammy laughed. "Oops, he got away. I'm sorry."

"Sammy," begged Mrs. Crabtree, "please see me. Harley, your friend, is here with you. Speak to him."

"I'm sorry. Do you have to go back to sleep?" Sammy asked. "So do I... I have to go back to sleep." He closed his eyes; his arms dropped back down on the bed. Sammy went to sleep—again. Neither his mother nor his doctor could wake him. All the adults stepped into the hallway to discuss what had just happened.

"Sammy," whispered Harley, "wake up. Please."

Suddenly Sammy snatched his hand again. "I'll wait for you, Harley," he said without opening his eyes. "Hurry, Harley."

Harley Delosian was taken aback by what had happened between Sammy and him. He decided not to share Sammy's message with the adults in the hall. However, on the way home he told TJ, Azlynn, and Tamiko everything.

"Where does he want you to go?" Tamiko asked.

"I don't know," Harley said.

"Who is Epiman—whatever?" Azlynn asked.

"He said Epimend," Harley corrected, "and I don't know who he is."

"Are you sure he was chasing a crow?" TJ asked. "Why a crow?"

"He made it sound like both he and that other person were chasing the bird," Harley explained. "I don't know why it was a crow."

"He said that both he and Epimend had to go back to sleep," TJ repeated. "That's kind of strange."

"It was strange," Harley agreed. "He was squeezing my hand so hard that I think he was afraid to let go."

That night Harley went online to research Epimend, but it came up as Epimenides, a Greek poet/philosopher who was born in the year 659 BC. Harley found the entries to be difficult to understand. Several talked about the Epimenides Paradox. It didn't make any sense to Harley. It kept saying that all Cretans are liars. He found a story about how Epimenides saved Athens by cleaning up the pollution. Finally, different entries disagreed on when and how Epimenides died.

Next, he searched the crow reference. As animal spirits, crows and ravens were often mentioned together. Harley learned that on one hand, crows were considered good luck; on the other, they were often called tricksters and shape-shifters. Exhausted, he finally closed out the screen. He, too, had to go to sleep.

It was late. Just as Harley began drifting off, he heard Stephen Colbert on his late night show announce Jon Batiste and the Stay

Human Band with their jazzy rendition of the Beatles' "Blackbird." He smiled. "Goodnight, Sammy," he mumbled.

"Blackbird fly, blackbird fly into the light of the dark black night."

His dream was haunted by Batiste's deep, mellow voice calling the blackbirds. His head was filled with harsh caws and deep throaty croaks all around him. He found himself flying on the back of a giant blackbird, probably a raven. Joining them was a murder of crows, soaring frantically all around them.

The huge blackbird cocked its head and said, "You have to hurry, Harley." Then it swooped downward and raced across an expanse of moonlit sea. Landmasses of islands of all sizes shot past them. Harley held tightly to the black plumage of this magnificent bird.

"Where do I go?" Harley heard himself shout.

"Start at the beginning," the blackbird answered.

"I don't know where that is."

"You will know—soon," the bird told him. Then it did a barrel roll, knocking Harley from its back. "Tell no lies," the bird echoed as it flew off into the dead of night.

Harley landed on wooden planks jutting out into the dark sea. Off in the distance, he could see a similar structure.

"Look, Harley," a childlike voice laughed, "a true pair of docks!" He could make out the sounds of a sheep or goat herd, but he could see nothing in the blackness beyond.

"All Cretans are liars," someone announced. "Are you a liar, Harley?"

Confused and becoming concerned that he was not alone, Harley strained to find someone, anyone, but he was alone. Something strange was happening inside his body, inside his mind. There was a kind of shift in energy that he could not define. He felt fearless.

Suddenly, out of nowhere, Sammy and Ms. Clio stood before him in blazing sunlight.

"Hurry, Harley," said Ms. Clio. The grains of sand stop for no man."

"You can do it, Harley," Sammy encouraged. "You will find a way."

Huge grains of sand fell one by one out of the sky above him. As each one hit, the ground beneath his feet rumbled.

"Which way?" Harley shouted.

"It's right in front of you, Harley," Ms. Clio promised. "Open your eyes."

"Harley," a familiar voice called, "Harley Delosian, open your eyes. You are going to be late for school," Valoria Delosian scolded her sleepy son.

"Aw, Mom," Harley complained. "I just got to sleep."

"What's this?" she asked, picking up a glossy black feather from Harley's floor. "Are you taking up ornithology now?"

Harley could only stare at the feather. He didn't understand any of it.

"Hurry up, Harley," his mother ordered. "Breakfast will be on the table in ten minutes."

CHAPTER 11

Interpretation

"Let us continue with the constellations and mythological characters for which many of you were named," announced Ms. Clio. "You should already have the story behind Ursa Major and Ursa Minor in your notes. Are there any lingering questions regarding yesterday's lesson?" She looked across the room. "Azlynn?"

"I just have a comment," Azlynn offered. "It bothers me that Hera, the Queen of the Universe, took out her anger on the mortal woman and her innocent son. Why didn't she confront Zeus? He started it all."

"That's a very astute observation, Azlynn," Ms. Clio began. "Remember, the ancient Greeks created their gods in their own likeness in both appearance and behavior. Do you think modern people behave similarly?"

"What do you mean?" a girl next to Azlynn asked.

"Have you noticed that if a girl, for whatever reason, draws the attention of a young man who is seriously dating another girl, the girlfriend tends not to confront her boyfriend, but rather, she goes after the other girl?" Ms. Clio said. "Why do you think that happens?"

Several students raised their hands. "I think it's because she doesn't want to risk losing the boyfriend."

"I think she knows she can intimidate the other girl."

Jacob Rogers had a totally different take on the situation. "I think girls are just crazy and if I were that guy I'd dump both of them."

Ms. Clio smiled. "However, as human beings, we thrive on companion-ship—that of family, community, or through romantic relationships. So, the Greeks attributed the same need for company to their gods."

Jacob couldn't resist. "I still think girls are crazy. Nobody understands why they do the things they do."

Ms. Clio noticed that Harley was not engaged in the discussion. Something was bothering him. She'd try to draw him out after school.

"Let us move on to groups of mythological characters," she suggested eagerly. "There are the Three Sisters of Fate who spin, dispense, and cut the threads of life; the Gorgon sisters of whom Medusa with her serpent hair is the most famous; and the less ominous Muses and Graces." She wrote a list of names under each group. The class copied her notes and a few noticed that the Muse of History was called Clio.

"Were you named after that Muse?" Tamiko wondered out loud.

"You might say I was," the teacher said, winking in fun.

"Ms. Clio," another student reminded her, "you said that you were going to tell us about the Seven Sisters, the Pleedees."

"Thank you, they are called the Pleiades," Ms. Clio said, writing the names on the board. "*Plein* means to sail. Pleione, the sailing queen, is said to be the mother of the Seven Sisters, and Atlas, their father. The location of the sun in the spring and in the fall determined the sailing season for the ancient Greeks."

She drew a genealogical tree showing family connections. "Pleione was an Oceanid, or daughter or Oceanus and Tethys, the Titans who ruled the seas before it was given to Poseidon."

Ms. Clio turned to address the class. As she spoke, she strode over to Harley's desk. She pointed to the blank page in front of him, reminding him to take notes. "Please keep in mind that some characters have more than one name and that a name can be attached to more than one character. The myths were passed on to each generation through word of mouth. Just like you and I do, they perhaps tended to embellish the parts they liked and ignore those they found uninteresting or disturbing."

Harley made an effort to focus, but couldn't take his mind off his dream and Sammy's request. Ms. Clio continued naming the Seven Sisters and drawing lines connecting their important family relationships to the gods. He heard only bits and pieces.

"Alcyone was called the queen who wards off storms; Asterope gave birth to the Sirens who sang so beautifully that sailors were lured to their deaths; Celaeno was the dark-skinned sister who was struck by a lightning bolt; Electra was named for the alloy of silver and gold and in Latin her name means *amber*; Maia was the eldest, the grandmotherly persona and the most beautiful—who gave birth to Hermes, the Messenger God; Merope was the bee-eater who marries a mortal; and finally, Taygete, the long-necked sister who gave birth to the founder of Sparta, Lacedaemon."

"Ms. Clio," a student said, "why are six of those stars easy to see, but the seventh one…well, I can hardly find it?"

"Some say it is Electra who hid her face at the fall of Troy," Ms. Clio explained. It's hard to say for sure which of the Seven Sisters fades into the night sky."

She ended the day's lesson by telling the class that the great hunter Orion fell in love with one or all of the Pleiades and practically stalked them. Mighty Zeus turned the sisters into doves and placed them in the sky as the train of Artemis. She outlined another constellation with her pointer. "Zeus also placed Orion in the sky so that the Pleiades were just out of his reach."

The final bell sounded. Once again the discussion among the students continued out into the hall. "Excuse me," Ms. Clio said, intercepting Harley. "I need you and your friends to stay after today."

TJ, Tamiko, and Azlynn agreed immediately. Harley, who had hardly spoken a word, spoke up, "Am I in trouble? I'm sorry I wasn't paying attention today. I've got things on my mind."

"And that's why I asked you to stay." Ms. Clio moved to the large table in the back of the room. The friends joined her. "Okay, now," she began, "tell me what's going on."

Harley narrated everything that had happened at the hospital. His friends nodded in agreement. "Do you know why Sammy went back to sleep?" asked TJ.

"I have an idea," Ms. Clio said. "Let Harley finish his telling his story."

"That's all that happened, Ms. Clio," Azlynn proclaimed.

"No, my dear, I think Harley has more to tell us." She turned to Harley.

"I haven't told you guys about my dream," Harley said. "I was waiting for after school."

"It's after school, Harley," Tamiko said. "Tell us."

Harley told them about his research, about Epimenides, and about the blackbirds. "You were in my dream, Ms. Clio. You were standing with Sammy and telling me to open my eyes."

It was obvious to everyone at the table that Harley was troubled and confused. The students turned to their teacher. "Can you help us, Ms. Clio?" asked TJ.

"I might have some explanations for you, but I don't have all the answers."

She told them the story behind Epimenides. "When he was a boy herding sheep or goats, he fell asleep in a cave, a special cave. When he awoke, 50 years had passed and the world had changed. So had Epimenides changed. Apollo, the god of prophecy, had given him special gifts while he slept. Epimenides had become a seer; some say he only saw the past; others say he was one of Seven Wise Poets in ancient Greece. Apollo was known for telling the truth; Epimenides became a poet and a philosopher who challenged the idea of what truth really meant."

She could tell that her explanation was too much for these twelve-year-olds. "Epimenides, like the American folk hero Rip Van Winkle, slept for a long time. Sammy spoke about having to go back to sleep because he didn't catch the crow."

"What does the crow have to do with this?" Harley asked.

"The *Korvus*, or crow, is Apollo's bird. It used to be white, but it made the mistake of giving Apollo bad news, and later, of lying to him. In anger, Apollo blasted the bird with his fiery flash and scorched him black."

Tamiko raised her hand and then realized class was over. "Why do you think Sammy and that Greek boy were chasing the crow?"

"It all relates to Apollo," Ms. Clio told them, "and you know, Apollo holds dominion over medicine."

TJ sat up straight. "Do you think Apollo can heal Sammy?"

"That's it—isn't it, Ms. Clio," Harley suddenly realized. "Sammy's concussion sleep and the 50-year sleep of Epimenides are both related to Apollo." He looked long and hard at his friends. "I have to find that crow who will lead me to Apollo who can heal Sammy."

"Harley!" Azlynn snapped, wanting to argue the point.

"No, Azlynn," Harley went on, "Sammy told me to hurry."

"Ms. Clio," TJ finally spoke louder than the others, "do you know how to help us so that we can help Sammy?"

Ms. Clio looked thoughtfully at each eager young face. She had to be very careful. What she chose to do next would make all the difference. "I might be able to find out something for you," she promised. "Tomorrow—after school."

CHAPTER 12

Heroes

"Why are you in that boy's head?" Clio asked her cousin.

"What do you mean?" Apollo defended himself.

"You put him in contact with your mortal Epimenides. You placed your crow in his head…in his head…why?" Clio was frustrated. "These mortals need our help, not more confusion."

"I'm trying to help you, Clio," he explained. "I know how you feel about those young mortals. I have watched you guide them closer to believing."

"So you sabotage my efforts by filling their heads with things they don't understand?" She turned away from his ever-growing shine. Whenever Apollo became agitated, his brilliant aura turned into a fiery glow. "Are you doing this on your own or do you have others with you who want to see me fail?"

"Clio, you've got it all wrong," he began to explain his actions. "There are several of us who want you to succeed. We want to have a greater influence on human lives. Just like in their old *Star Trek* episode, we don't want to fade away into oblivion."

"You have an odd way of showing this."

"We have to be careful," Apollo went on. "Zeus has forbidden us to participate in your classroom at this time. If we do, then your quest is over and you must return to Olympus immediately."

An even wiser cousin, Pallas Athena, who was born from Zeus's head, appeared. Her owl joined her. "Cousins," she greeted, "it seems Clio has a problem."

"I do, Athena; I need help to prove to the Olympian Council that mortals do believe—that we non-mortals do matter to them."

"I am aware of your dilemma," Athena said. "I have an idea that might help you and help them."

She went on to explain that the sleeping boy was doomed never to wake unless his friends could quench his thirst from the Cup of Hygea.

"You cannot interfere in human affairs, Muse Clio; you can teach, you can guide, and you can explain, but you cannot directly participate in their decisions." Athena knew the mind of her father well. Although he was not omniscient, all-knowing, he did seem to find out about those who broke his edicts. The entire Olympian world knew just how harsh the punishments were for defying his orders.

"The friends would have to enter our world to secure the cup," Clio said.

"Yes, cousin," Apollo replied, "and they would be in a different world and a different time."

"You could help them," Clio said excitedly.

"We can never make their decisions," he declared, "but we can do things along the way that could cause them to make correct choices.

"I will provide the road map throughout our world," Athena offered. "I will pass it to them through your mortal Epimenides."

"I will set before them a means to travel from one place to another," Apollo said. "It will be up to them to recognize the opportunity."

"We can talk with the others about how they could eventually get the cup and take it to Sammy." Clio paced nervously. Out loud she worried, "These mortals must not be injured. Before a fatal blow—before a critical misstep—before the horrid sister of Fate, Atropos, snips their life threads, they must be returned to their world."

"Agreed," Athena said, stroking her pet owl.

"You have such faith in them," Apollo noted. "I have yet to witness their bravery. They must prove their merit in the choices they make and their bravery in following through no matter the cost. You must not tell them that they will be safe in their journey. Such news will alter their choices."

"I understand," Clio agreed. "I have to return and educate them about our world. I mean really educate them."

"Beware of the brothers of the lower world, Sleep and Death," warned Apollo. "They may send Dreams through the ivory gate which will give your mortals false thoughts. That could prove dangerous."

"Morpheus must be behind this as well," added Athena. "In his father's abode near the black country of the Cimmerians, where the only sound is that of the stream called Lethe, the river of forgetfulness, Morpheus plots against the alert. He can change his form to that of any human. Your charges should know that about him."

"This could prove troublesome to the young mortals," Clio said. "I must find a way for them to know him."

That night Ms. Clio rewrote her lesson plans for Humanities I. She decided to set aside the constellations and introduce more earthly stories about the gods and other mythological creatures. The more information these mortal children had, the greater their chances for a successful journey.

The next day in class, Ms. Clio began by listing several Greek names on the whiteboard. Above the list she wrote: "*DEMI-GODS.*"

"These are mortals, many of whom have divine blood in their veins. Even if there be no proof of a royal bloodline, these mythological beings demonstrate honor, heroism, loyalty, and wisdom beyond ordinary men. They are probably mankind's closest link to his gods. They were called heroes back then. Even today, people you identify as being heroes stand out among the masses."

She read through the list of some of the heroes before the Trojan War: "Perseus—Theseus—Herakles (aka Hercules)—Atalanta."

The students were anxious to follow her of thinking. "Atalanta is descended from Prometheus, the Titan. Perseus and Hercules are sons of mortal mothers and the great Zeus. And finally, Theseus. Although his deeds were truly heroic, there is no divine blood in him."

TJ raised his hand. "What did they do to make them heroes?"

"Perseus destroyed Medusa, the Gorgon with serpent hair and a deadly stare."

"I saw the movie," Tamiko reported. "Her body was like a snake, and if any man looked into her eyes, he was turned to stone."

"Yes, it was her punishment for boasting aloud about her beautiful tresses, saying they surpassed the beauty of Athena. Obviously, those once beautiful locks were transformed into hissing serpents. Scattered throughout her miserable cavern were petrified men and animals that chanced a glimpse at her horrible face.

"What did the only girl on the list do?" asked Azlynn.

"Because Atalanta was not born a boy, her disappointed father left her to die on a mountainside. A she-bear saved her. Later, kind hunters found her and raised her. She grew stronger and more clever than most of the young men around her. She eventually defeated the vicious Calydonian boar that had been ravaging the land. A band of strong young men came first to kill the boar. Atalanta joined them in the hunt. Some thought it beneath them to hunt with a woman. In the confusion, she kept her head and inflicted the first wound. The king's son, who was enamored of her, inflicted the last wound. He insisted that Atalanta be honored with the skin. He would eventually die as a result of that decision."

Another boy raised his hand, "That story doesn't seem very heroic to me."

Azlynn went on the attack. "Are you kidding me? Women weren't allowed to do anything but tend to the home and raise children. For her to step outside that…that," she struggled for the right words, "that stereotype, was braver than cutting off the head of a monster."

"Let's not get into a gender war," Ms. Clio interrupted. "The point of that matter is that heroes go above and beyond what is expected of ordinary men…and women."

Ms. Clio circled the name Hercules. "He was a flawed hero. Just like most men he had his strengths and his shortcomings. Because Zeus was his father, Hercules became the subject of Hera's vengeful nature. In a fit of enchanted rage cast by Hera, he killed his beloved wife and children. For years on end, he punished himself by performing twelve labors, tasks that no mere mortal could ever achieve."

Harley listened intently. These stories aroused his imagination. He was feeling a sense of power. It was as if something inexplicable was streaming through the ether regions of space into his body. It was a good feeling. No—it was a great feeling.

"Ms. Clio," he began, "what about Theseus?"

"Oh," she smiled. "He was the greatest of all Athenians. His heroic triumph was that of destroying the Minotaur who lived in the great Labyrinth of Daedalus on the isle of Crete, ruled by King Minos. The half-bull, half-man creature pursued and devoured the fourteen Athenian youths and maidens who were locked inside the Labyrinth as yearly sacrificial tribute to King Minos. Theseus, though a prince, joined the next group of fourteen with one objective in mine—slaying the Minotaur.

"Wow," Harley said, sitting up taller and breathing deeper. "That had to take selfless courage. Theseus was a real hero."

CHAPTER 13

Time and Space

In a clandestine gathering after school, the four friends met with Ms. Clio once again. Sammy had not awakened since Harley's visit to his hospital room. What he was doing, however, was talking with someone as if he were a close friend. He'd laugh and chatter as if he and his unseen friend were having the time of their lives. During these episodes Mrs. Crabtree held him tightly to her body as if he might disappear from her at any moment.

"Ms. Clio," Azlynn began the discussion, "Sammy doesn't seem sick or broken—he's acting as if he is in another world. Why?"

"The brain is a complex organ whose mysteries modern science has yet to fully unravel," explained the teacher. "We may never really know what's going on in his mind."

Harley jumped into the conversation. "If he were living in the ancient world, what would they say is happening to him?"

"The ancient healers might say that he has been influenced by Morpheus, the God of Sleep. His offspring scour every corner of the earth searching for spirited souls who will become companions for him in his state of slumber. Sammy is a spirited soul; perhaps Morpheus wants him to join his terrible family."

"That's awful, Ms. Clio," cried Tamiko. "We love Sammy. We don't want him to go away."

"Modern medicine has no power over ancient curses," Ms. Clio said.

"Is there an ancient cure that could wake Sammy up?" asked TJ.

"The daughter of Apollo's son is said to possess a medicinal bowl that can cure any ailment of anyone who drinks from it," explained Clio. "You see, one of Apollo's domains is the ability to heal. He taught those skills to Chiron, the rejected offspring of a sea-nymph and Kronos, the father of the original Olympians. Chiron's mother tried to escape Kronos by shifting into a mare and running away. Consequently, Chiron was born half-man, half-horse, a centaur, but he was different, kinder and more intellectual than other centaurs. He grew to be a teacher. Among his students were Jason of the Argonauts; Theseus, the future king of Athens; Achilles, hero of Troy; and Aesculapius, the son of Apollo. Aesculapius became the embodiment of the healing practices. He passed his knowledge to his daughter Hygea."

"So was Hygea—like a doctor?" Tamiko asked.

"Maybe she was the first female doctor," added Azlynn.

"Hygea does become the Goddess of Health," said Ms. Clio. "From her name that is sometimes spelled *Hygia*, we get our word *hygiene*."

"Tell us about her cup or bowl," Harley said. He was eager to understand how this ancient object might help Sammy. A greater concern for Harley was just how they were going to get a hold of it.

Ms. Clio related the ancient cup to a modern pharmaceutical symbol. "The top graduate from one pharmaceutical college is awarded a replica of Hygea's Cup. Imagine a shiny cup with delicately carved snakes entwined around the stem and wrapped around the bowl."

"Snakes!" shrieked Azlynn. "Why snakes?"

"There's a myth about how Aesculapius, Hygea's father, once killed a snake. As it lay dead, he watched another snake place an herb on the dead snake's open mouth. This herb brought the dead snake back to life and both snakes slithered away together. Aesculapius was astounded and knew exactly what to do. He began using the same herb to bring men back to life. He was so successful that Hades, the God of the Underworld where all deceased spirits must go, complained to Zeus, who chose to strike Aesculapius with a thunder-bolt, killing him. Apollo, the father of Aesculapius, begged Zeus to reconsider. So, Zeus lifted Aesculapius into the heavens to live among the stars."

People had worshipped Aesculapius and built temples in his honor. The sick would come to these temples and sleep in rows along the walls. Some said Aesculapius and his daughters would bring medicines to the sick. Others said that the snakes who lived under the floors of these temples would come out at night and lick the wounds of the sick, healing them. In the morning, the healed people would drop cakes into the snake holes as offerings of thanks."

"Were these temples like hospitals?" TJ asked.

"Maybe," Ms. Clio offered, "but throughout history people have gone to churches or temples seeking cures for their physical ailments as well as the spiritual pain."

Harley got excited. "We need to get the cup!"

"You mean," Tamiko said, "a cup *like* the one Hygea had."

"I don't think that's what he means," TJ said. "He means we have to get that cup."

"Does it even exist any more?" Azlynn asked with skepticism. "Ms. Clio, does it?"

Ms. Clio looked at each of her students. "It exists in the mythological world of the ancient Greeks."

TJ thought for a moment before speaking. "Ms. Clio, we know who you are." Ms. Clio tried to stop him. "You live in two worlds and that's okay with us. I have already told them about my fuzzy head feeling and Harley told us about the changes that he experienced during the discussion about the heroes. The girls believe us even though they haven't had any experiences like Harley and me…yet."

Cutting to the chase, Harley announced, "We've got to go back to that world, get the cup, and save Sammy."

Their minds were made up. All they needed to know was how to accomplish this quest.

"Such a journey will be very difficult and extremely dangerous," warned Ms. Clio. "Mortals wiser and more experienced than you have become lost attempting such a journey."

"This would be like time travel," decided Azlynn. "I've read a lot of stories about it."

Harley was all ready to go. "We have to find a way in and make sure we can get back."

"Yeah," TJ agreed. "We need to know exactly where to go in the ancient world."

"And we will need to know how to get around once we get there," added Azlynn.

"We don't look like the ancient Greeks," Tamiko reminded them. "We would stand out like a sore thumb."

"Greek children generally wore a slip-on garment and sandals," Ms. Clio said, continuing her instruction. "The boys wore a loincloth and a headband to keep their long hair out of their eyes." She looked hard at the group. "Not all of you can cross over," Clio warned. "It would be too difficult to track your progress and bring all of you back safely."

"How many can go?" TJ asked.

"I think two of us should go and two of us should protect the gateway," Harley suggested. "We'll decide and let you know."

"I'll get some maps of the topography of ancient Greece so we can study them," Azlynn offered.

"So, I'll bring my survival manual, and we can study those things we might need to know in a world without smartphones, TV, and the Internet."

"How long does a journey like this take?" Tamiko wanted to know.

"I have no way of knowing," Ms. Clio told them solemnly. "It could be minutes or it could be years." She saw the fear in their eyes. "The ancients did not perceive time in the same way you do. Time is a massive, extraordinarily soft, nearly invisible blanket that can be folded upon itself—layer upon layer. They believed that if you know the secrets of time and space, you can move from layer to layer because time and space are limitless—having no beginning and no end. Albert Einstein came very close to understanding the secrets of time and space. Eventually, the memory of the previous time fades into finite particles the longer one stays in the new time."

"Now," Harley said, "I understand why this journey could be very, very dangerous."

CHAPTER 14

FEATHERS

The last period of the day on Friday was dedicated to First Quarter celebration. All of the students gathered in the gym; each grade level sat in designated sections. The JFK Student Council and Principal Homer ran the assembly. The Pledge was recited and the school song sung.

"I'd like to begin today's celebration by congratulating the 8th grade class for having the highest grade point average this quarter. You will enjoy ice cream sundaes in the lunchroom after this ceremony. The 8th graders earned an average of 3.8 overall, with the 7th graders right behind with a 3.6 average."

The principal paused, giving the students time to cheer for themselves.

"Sixth graders, your 3.0 average is no small achievement. However, I'm positive that if you put your collective noses to the grindstone, you can surpass the 7th and 8th graders."

The 6th graders cheered loudly; the rest of the student body booed them back into their seats. Following the spirit squad's performance, the principal stepped to the microphone one more time.

"And congratulations to the Strikers soccer team for winning the Divisional Championship—again…" Principal Homer tried to continue, but the raucous cheering for the Strikers roared on.

Finally, raising a hand in the air, Principal Homer brought the entire gymnasium to silence.

"I know it has been difficult for this team because one of their teammates remains in the hospital. I am fully aware that at least one Striker has visited his hospital room every day since the accident. For this I commend your loyalty and deep sense of friendship. An eagle feather with your names on it as members of the Strikers will be hung on our Celebration Wall in recognition of your devotion and true team spirit."

Once again, the room erupted in whoops and whistles. Harley Delosian was called to the podium to accept the feather of honor on behalf of his team.

"Thank you, Principal Homer," he said to the entire room. "The Strikers are the greatest."

TJ and the girls noticed that Harley did not smile. At Sammy's bedside last night, he had learned that Sammy was becoming less exuberant. The doctor had told Mrs. Crabtree that the prognosis for his recovery was now less than 50%. Harley had no reason to smile.

"Next," Principal Homer continued, "I'd like to call up the following students who will also receive an eagle feather. "Thomas Harris, 7th grade…" the principal called four more names. TJ and the others rose and shyly strode to the middle of the room. This eagle feather tradition was highly respected across the school.

"You deserve it," Harley said to his friend. "You are one of the nicest guys in this school."

"Thanks, Harley," TJ said, "but we've got bigger things to think about."

"I know," Harley returned. "Ms. Clio is expecting us after school. We're going to go tomorrow; Sammy's getting worse. There's no time to waste."

The foursome sat around the table with their Humanities teacher. They had made their decision about who was going to go to the other side and who was going to guard the gateway.

"It only makes sense, Ms. Clio," said Azlynn. "I've been reading about what life was like back then—and—well, since boys had greater freedom to explore than girls—who were expected to stay home—we decided that Harley and TJ have a better chance of completing the task."

"I think your reasoning is sound," Ms. Clio said. "It would be unusual for girls to be running around unsupervised."

"We want to go tomorrow," TJ told her. "So, if there's anything else we need to know, now is the time to tell us."

"You have read the myths; you have studied the maps; and you have a general understanding of the Minoan culture and the Mycenaean culture." Ms. Clio was still worried. These were children, but children in those cultures were far more independent and sometimes more brutal than modern children. Adults in those communities would be about their business; they would hardly notice two more boys among them. The Minoan and Mycenaean boys might spot them immediately. Challenges for superiority were bound to occur. Harley and TJ had to be alert.

"You must arrive as does a newborn infant," she continued. "Never allow anyone to see you unclothed. Greek boys were not circumcised, and if you are, you would be perceived as a foreigner—a possible threat—and that would be dangerous."

"Well, what do we do?" Harley asked, a little embarrassed about the topic.

"You will go directly to Apollo's cave to retrieve your ancient supplies," she explained. "Your guide will meet you there."

"Our guide?" TJ repeated. "Who is our guide?"

"I cannot say," she answered. "Events on the other side are being arranged by someone else." She reached inside her pocket and pulled out two unusual amulets on leather thongs. "These are from the other side," she said, holding them in the air, "but because I brought them across, they are safe for you to take with you when you cross over."

"What are they," Tamiko spoke up, "tracking devices?"

"In the ancient world, infants who survived the first five days were celebrated in a ceremony called the Amphidromia. At this time, relatives bearing gifts came to welcome the infant into the *oikos*, or family household.

The gifts were intended to prevent misfortune, ward off demons, and keep the evil eye from looking at the child. These are your charms; wear them the entire time you are over there, but you must leave them behind when you return."

Harley and TJ held up the amulets. They were flattened pieces of metal that looked like a coin. Along the edge two snakes seemed to undulate after each other. In the center on one side was an owl image. On the back, the unsettling gaze of a black crow looked back at them.

Harley looked to Ms. Clio. Without saying a word, she knew he understood.

The crow brought Apollo's wisdom and the owl brought Athena's strength. The snakes would guide him to toward their destination. He smiled and slipped the pendant over his head.

"There's one last thing," TJ reminded the group, "how do we find the gateway to cross over?"

"In a place of your own, where the four of you feel safe, you will cause the gateway to open. That's when you two step through. Tamiko, Azlynn, you two must maintain that spot so that nothing changes, allowing them to come back at the space place."

She gave them time to consider multiple locations.

"The gateway will remain open for 3 minutes only," she warned them. "If you sit in a union, a circle, it will open in the center."

"Does it hurt to go through?" Azlynn asked.

"No, the journey to the other side will feel like the blink of an eye. However, the landing may be a bit bumpy."

Tamiko continued, "Is it the same coming back?"

"Harley and TJ will form their own circle using their charms which they must leave behind when they step through."

Harley scratched his head. "Will we know if we have done everything we were supposed to do over there?"

"Harley," Ms. Clio said, "TJ, trust your own instincts. You will not only see and hear things that will be unfamiliar to you, but you will feel a sensation deep inside you. Depend on each other; trust each other. More than I will be watching your journey every step of the way."

PART TWO

The Quest

Chapter 15

The Crossing

"You realize that you guys don't even know what you're really after," Azlynn complained. "That worries me. How will you know where to go and what to get?"

"Relax, Azlynn," Harley answered. "I know you're nervous for us, but I believe that once we arrive there, we will know everything we need to know to finish the job."

"I'm scared," Tamiko told the group while she hugged Apollo tightly. "I'm scared that you might get hurt and be unable to get back."

TJ patted Apollo's head. "As long as we stay together, we can form our own gateway and come home."

"Then stay together—no matter what," ordered Tamiko.

The four friends decided that the fort in Harley's backyard would be their safe place. It was built high among the branches of a very large old tree. They had built a lift so that Apollo could join them in the fort.

"I wish that you could be with us," Harley confessed. "You have read every book you could find about the ancient Greek world."

"Well, I've tried to tell you guys things about the time and the places that might impact your journey," Azlynn said. "I just hope you remember them when you need them."

"We'll be all right," TJ promised. "Just be here so that we can find our way back."

"And you, buddy," Harley said to Apollo, "you bark loudly so I can hear you on the other side. Then I'll know everything's okay."

The boys traded their usual clothes for large beach towels that were wrapped tightly around them.

"Remember," TJ told the girls, "you have to close your eyes when the gateway opens. When you don't hear us, then you can open them again."

The girls looked at each other nervously. Only in science fiction had anyone dared to cross into another dimension.

Harley recognized their almost tearful expressions. "Sammy needs us to do this," he said. "If we don't, who will help him?"

"We love Sammy," Azlynn said firmly, "and we know we're doing the right thing."

"But that doesn't mean we're not scared," finished Tamiko.

"Let's get going," TJ urged the group.

They sat in a circle and joined hands. No one in the group had any idea what would happen next.

"Let's close our eyes and clear our minds," suggested TJ. That fuzzy feeling was beginning to vibrate. "It won't be long."

It was a matter of seconds before the air around them felt thick and fluid. They opened their eyes. The circle they made with their bodies was rolling like gentle waves. Next, the wavy air began to swirl. As they watched in amazement, the center opened into a bottomless pit of blackness.

"That's it!" Harley shrieked. "Close your eyes!"

Apollo barked fiercely, trying to pull away from Tamiko. The boys dropped their towels, glanced at each other, reaffirming their determination, grabbed the amulets, and jumped. Apollo barked wildly. Exactly three minutes later, the air was back to normal; the gateway was gone…so were the boys.

"Let's draw a chalk circle right here," Tamiko suggested. "I want to mark the gateway exactly."

"Good idea," agreed Azlynn. "This is crazy—just crazy."

Afraid he might accidentally fall through an invisible hole, they leashed Apollo and ordered him to lie down next to their hastily drawn circle. The girls prepared to pass the time with books, drawing, and various games. Every few minutes they glanced at the circle, looking for changes.

Inside the passage, all the boys could hear was air being sucked out of what seemed like a massive tube. They were pulled hard. Within seconds, brilliants light flashed below them, and then, THUMP! They hit the ground with a thud.

"Ouch!" shouted Harley.

"You okay, Harley?"

"I'm going to have a bruise on my butt," he said, rubbing his behind.

TJ laughed. "You look funny; your hair is standing straight up." TJ's closely-cropped hair was also on end, but it was barely noticeable. They stood up as naked as the day they were born. Embarrassed that they were standing in a strange place without a stitch of clothing, they covered themselves and began searching for a cave—Apollo's cave.

"Look there," TJ said. "That looks like a hilly area where a cave might be."

"Let's climb that way, then," Harley said.

Neither boy noticed that the serpents on their amulets were pointing in the same direction they had chosen to follow. Their quest had begun.

"I heard Apollo barking," Harley said as they worked their way up the hill."

"Me, too," TJ said. "He's really loud and I'm kinda glad about that."

The tall grass covering the hillside scratched at their bare skin. The sun shone brightly and seemed closer to earth than what the boys thought was natural. They saw people in the distance and did everything they could not to be seen.

"Look," Harley said, pointing upward. "There *is* a cave up there."

The closer they got to the hole in the hillside, the more the pathway cleared. Without the tall grass for cover, they began to sprint toward the opening.

"I hope it's the right cave," TJ cried, out of breath. "There were several other gaping holes across the hills surrounding them.

"We'll search them all if we have to," Harley said. "One of them has to be Apollo's."

As they approached the first opening, the serpents on their amulets returned to their original position. In the mythic world, Apollo frowned. "Keep your eyes open, young mortals. Don't miss the clues that lie before you."

Harley and TJ ran eagerly into the first cave opening. The cavern was shallow and empty. Once again, the serpents became animated and stretched northward. This time TJ saw Harley's amulet move.

"Harley," he said, stopping in his tracks. "Look!"

Harley followed his pointed finger to the metal disk that lay on his chest. Both heads were pointing in the same direction. "Yours is moving, too," he said to TJ.

"Could they be a compass?" TJ asked.

"Let's move and check them."

The boys climbed to the next opening. The snakes pointed in the opposite direction. "Let's go check out that one," said Harley. As they moved to the obvious opening, the snakes turned their heads to the left. "There's nothing there," he said, disappointed and tired. "Why are they pointing that way?"

Despite his fatigue, TJ became insistent. "Harley, this isn't our world. We have to trust the guides that have been sent to us. Maybe these snakes are guides." He began a precarious climb toward a nearly hidden depression on the hillside. Trudging several yards through prickly bushes, TJ yelled in triumph.

"It's here, Harley! There's an opening."

Unlike the other caves whose entrances seemed to have been hollowed out, this cave opening was nothing more than a crack in the rocks. The fissure was just wide enough for a small child to pass through. TJ was the first inside.

Slowly, his eyes adjusted to the shadowy hue of the cavern. Cool air wafted from deep inside the hole. The entrance was deceptive.

"Wow," Harley swallowed. "This has to be Apollo's cave."

On a large, flattened boulder, the boys found two sets of authentic garb, including sandals. The bottoms of their feet were tender; they were not accustomed to the rough terrain, so the footgear was greatly appreciated.

"What do I do with this?" Harley asked, holding up a long strip of fabric.

"Just wrap it around like a figure eight and tuck it in," TJ demonstrated. Now, he felt more normal. The essential parts of his body were properly covered.

"What do we do now?" Harley asked after wrapping himself as well, lacing his sandals up his calves.

"We wait," TJ said.

The owls on their amulets blinked twice.

CHAPTER 16

Arrival

"I'm really thirsty," Harley shared.

"Me, too," TJ coughed. "How long have we been here?"

"I don't know," Harley said, "but it feels like hours."

A rustling sound of animals filled the cavern. "We're not alone," Harley whispered. They heard the gentle commands of a young boy settling his herd.

"*Geia!*" he yelled through the opening.

Harley and TJ heard, "Hello!"

"Hello!" Harley yelled back.

The boy on the outside heard, "Geia!" He answered, "*To ónóma mou eínai Epimenides.*"

"TJ," whispered Harley, "it's him, Sammy's friend from his dreams."

"Epimenides, hello," TJ called happily. "My name is TJ."

No matter what language came out of their mouths, their ears heard their native tongue. They could communicate effortlessly.

"I brought you food and water," Epimenides said. "Come on out."

The two visitors squeezed between the rocks again. Standing in the clearing were several goats and a thin-framed Greek boy holding a long stick and a cloth bulging with food. He handed TJ a skin-bag filled with water. Harley drank eagerly before passing the bag to TJ. Most children have a way about them that easily welcomes another without actually saying anything.

Epimenides spread the cloth and separated the cheese and fruits he had packed. They ate and gesticulated satisfaction.

"I was really hungry and thirsty," TJ told the boy. "Thank you for bringing this to us."

"Did you know we were here?" Harley asked.

"I was told in a dream to bring food and water to Apollo's cave. At first I thought I was supposed to make a sacrifice to Apollo, but Korvus told me to feed the strangers."

"Korvus?" Harley asked, remembering Sammy's rantings in the hospital.

"Yes, he is Apollo's bird," Epimenides said proudly. "He talks to me all the time."

"Do you know Sammy?" Harley dared to ask.

"Aw, yes, my new friend Sammy Crab," the boy laughed delightedly. "He is too sick to play now."

"Sammy is our friend, too," TJ said proudly.

"Then we are all friends," Epimenides pronounced. "Korvus said I am to point the way, but I don't know the way to point to."

"Neither do we," Harley said. "We were hoping you had the answer."

The soft hooting of an owl sounded from across the clearing. "That's odd," Epimenides said, "Athena's bird usually comes out at night, but I clearly hear him."

"Me, too," TJ agreed. Both he and the boy worked their way toward the sound. "Harley, come quickly!" TJ yelled. "I found something."

On the ground beneath a low-hanging bush was a smoothly tooled leather pouch. Epimenides picked it up and tried to pull it apart, but the drawn opening would not give way. Next, TJ tried to open the pouch. He was successful. "Hey, there's nothing in here," he said disappointedly.

Harley took the pouch and looked inside. "What do you mean? It's not empty. There's some kind of hard paper, and it has writing on it." He pulled out a misshapen leathery paperlike object. The writing was totally foreign to Harley. "Can you read this?"

Epimenides held up the skin and began saying the words. As he spoke, the words turned into English alphabetic letters. Now Harley could read it himself.

"This is our first clue," he said, and began reading the message to TJ.

> Young mortals from lands beyond these shores.
>
> Prepare—the path you seek is now yours.
>
> Deviate not—its ordained route is set.
>
> If a cure is what you wish to get.
>
> Dare ye—enter the sorrowful maze.
>
> Where youth untouched consumed by craze.
>
> Retrieve the lifeline of Theseus.
>
> Present as a gift to Lachesis.

"Oh, my," muttered Epimenides, "that's not good."

"Why?" TJ asked.

"The maze is the Labyrinth where the savage Minotaur, son of King Minos, lives and dines on youthful Athenians."

"But the message says that if we don't go there, we can't help Sammy," Harley reminded them.

"Can you show us the way?" TJ asked.

"I can't leave my herd," Epimenides said, "but I can point you in the general direction. We're on an island, so you will eventually find it. Knossos is the main city. The Labyrinth of the Minotaur is there." He pointed south.

Epimenides embraced his new friends the way ancient Greeks did. They clasped forearms and nodded strongly. He handed them the goatskin of water and the remains of their lunch. "Have a safe journey, my friends," he said. "May Hermes guide and protect you as you travel and may Apollo light your way."

He turned away making clicking sounds to his grazing herd. Gently, he tapped their backs with his stick, encouraging them to move on. Harley and TJ watched as Epimenides, the boy who would fall asleep for 50 years, worked his herd across the next hill.

Harley returned the leathery parchment to the bag and turned southward. "Let's get going, TJ. I don't know how far away Knossos is." As they walked side by side in silence, Harley thought about Theseus, the Labyrinth, and the Minotaur.

Finally, Harley broke the silence, "TJ, tell me the myth of the Minotaur. Don't leave out any details, no matter how gruesome they might be."

The myth is really about the Athenian hero Theseus. The story begins when King Minos of Crete sent his son to Athens. The Cretan prince joined a perilous hunt for a bull. The hunt proved fatal for the prince. King Minos sent an army to raze Athens unless they agreed to send him a tribute of seven maidens and seven youths every nine years. These Athenians were placed in the Labyrinth, a maze constructed by the great architect Daedalus. There was no way out. They became victims of the horrific Minotaur, a half-man, half-bull creature—the stepson of King Minos and the half-brother of Princess Ariadne.

It was the ninth year again. Theseus, who had taken his place as Prince of Athens, insisted on being among the seven youths. When Theseus arrived in Crete along with the other tributes, he was paraded through the streets. It just so happened that Ariadne saw him and fell in love with him at first sight.

Ariadne asked the architect, Daedalus, to help her find a way to free Theseus from his certain death. She was able to speak secretly to Theseus before he entered the Labyrinth.

"If you promise to marry me," she said, "I will help you escape death at the hands of my brother."

Of course, Theseus promised to take her to Athens and marry her. She sent her nurse with a ball of thread that he could unravel as he wandered through the maze, and then follows its trail back to the gate to escape.

Theseus tied the thread to the gatepost and allowed it to unravel as he searched for the Minotaur. The other tributes ran wildly about the maze in sheer panic. He calmed them by telling them he would save them.

When he found the savage Minotaur, it was asleep. Theseus jumped upon it and beat it, because he had no weapons other than his wit and his fists. He killed the beast. The ball of twine lay in the spot where he'd dropped it. He followed the unraveled thread, collected the other Athenians, and took Ariadne to his ship.

All went well until he landed on the island of Naxos, where Ariadne fell asleep. His ship sailed away without her. Others say a storm blew him away from the shore of Naxos, and that when he was finally able to return, he found Ariadne dead.

Upon returning home, Theseus inadvertently hoisted the black sail, not the white sail that indicated success and safe return. The King of Athens saw the black sail, and stricken with unfathomable sorrow, he threw himself into the sea from the Acropolis and died. The sea became know as the Aegean, named for King Aegeus. Theseus then became king, and his rule would become known as the birth of democracy.

CHAPTER 17

The Entrance

"So according to the message," Harley thought aloud, "we have to get that ball of string."

"Yeah," agreed TJ, "and we have to deliver it Lachesis, the Fate sister who weaves the threads of life."

"I have no idea how to find her," Harley said, "but let's face that problem after we find the ball of string."

As they walked along a dirt road for at least an hour, Harley asked his friend about his vision of the Minotaur. "Do you think the body is that of a man or do you think his body is the bull?"

"Most pictures show him with the upper body and head of a bull, and the arms and legs of a man, but I've seen pictures that show it with four legs of a bull and the upper body of a very powerful man."

"If he had human arms, I guess he could rip apart his victims and eat them," Harley pondered the image.

"And by having a bull's legs, it would be able to chase down its victims easily," TJ added.

"But it would be scarier if he had the chest and head of a bull of and the arms and legs of a very big and strong man."

TJ thought about Harley's ideas. "Either way, he's a fierce monster hiding in a place that has no way out. That would be enough to scare me to death."

The boys could see the turquoise sheen of the Mediterranean Sea off in the distance. The air was truly fresh, with a strong hint of sea salt. They climbed another knoll and stopped at the top. Before them lay the magnificent city of Knossos.

"This has to be it. It's beautiful," Harley said.

"And it's big," added TJ.

They sat in the grass to eat the remains of their last meal. Harley surveyed the landscape.

"You know," TJ interrupted the silence, "the story goes on."

King Minos found out that Daedalus helped Theseus escape. He threw Daedalus and his son Icarus into the Labyrinth. Even for the designer, there was no earthly way out. So he devised wings for himself and his son to fly out over the walls.

"You must stay in the middle. Do not fly too high or the sun will melt the wax that holds your feathers to your wings," Daedalus warned.

As youth have done throughout the ages, Icarus did not listen to his father. He flew higher and higher, until Helios melted the wax, causing the arrogant boy to fall to his death. Daedalus did escape, finding sanctuary in another kingdom far from Crete.

King Minos devised a trick to find Daedalus. He promised a great reward to anyone who could thread a string through a spiraled shell. Of course, Daedalus could do this; he could not resist the challenge. He drilled a hole at one end, tied the thread to an ant, and squeezed it through the drilled hole. The ant came out the other end with the thread still tied to it.

King Minos had found Daedalus and ordered him returned to Crete. The sanctuary king refused, forcing Minos to bring an army to force the issue. This was an unfortunate decision. King Minos was killed in battle, and Daedalus stayed in his new land.

The travelers ate the food and drank from the waterskin until they were full. Yet, they still had leftovers, and the skin was not yet empty. As they rested, TJ recalled a lecture about the half-man, half-beast creatures in Greek mythology. "Remember what Ms. Clio said about Chiron?"

"What?"

"She said that centaurs are supposed to have the body of a horse and the torso and head of a man, but Chiron was different in many ways. He was not wild or violent like other centaurs. He was smart and civilized and his legs were human and his body was that of a horse."

"How does that work?" Harley asked. "I'm so confused. Let's go."

They walked down the incline. As they did, they began to feel different. TJ noticed a kind of wavy aspect, like that of a mirage in the desert. Harley seemed not to notice, so TJ chose to say nothing. At the edge of the city they saw a cluster of chiseled boulders lying in random piles. The path they followed forked in two directions. One seemed to lead to downtown Knossos, while the other disappeared into the cluster of stones.

TJ checked the amulet serpents. They were pointing to the right, the cluster of rocks. "That way," he pointed. Harley simply followed him without question. "Are you okay?"

"I'm fine," Harley snapped. "Let's get this done."

The entrance, no longer standing tall and foreboding, appeared as if a mortar shell had blasted its boulders and the massive timbers into a pile of rubble. The boys picked their way through the precariously stacked rocks, trying to avoid long, sharp slivers that protruded in every direction.

"Harley," called TJ, who was trying to follow his friend's pace over the rubble.

"Yeah," Harley answered. He was in the grip of determination. Finding that ball of thread was all he could focus on.

"This is worse than a pile of Pick-Up Sticks."

"Just step carefully, TJ," Harley warned. "We can't afford a twisted ankle or a deep cut. The opening is just ahead." He hopped over the boulders like an agile mountain goat.

If they could complete the challenges on this quest, Sammy might wake up for good. If they had to find their way to the center of what was left of the Minotaur's Labyrinth, they would it. Friendship motivated them; determination bolstered their spirits; youth gave them courage.

"I'm going to find that ball of string," Harley proclaimed.

At last they stood before the gaping mouth of the dreaded maze. A rancid breeze wafted from deep inside the cavern, causing the boys to cover their noses.

"Smells like the sewer when it backs up," Harley said. "Yuck!"

"Smells like death to me," TJ disagreed, "like those dead cats we found in the field last year."

"I remember," Harley said, "It was awful." He brushed away the image of a litter of kittens that were left to die at the edge of a big cornfield. Neither boy could understand why anyone would do such a thing to the tiny animals.

Harley's mom had told them, "Cruelty knows no bounds. Some people have no compassion and do mean and horrible things to innocent creatures." She went with them to the death place and helped the boys bury the litter of kittens. The memory was still hurtful; the very idea of senseless cruelty was haunting.

Harley and TJ faced each other. Theirs was the kind of friendship that didn't need a lot of conversation. Most of the time each knew what the other was thinking. As they stood motionless, the myth of King Minos and the Minotaur replayed in their minds. They were standing before what was left of the home of the bloodthirsty half-man, half-bull, cannibalistic monster.

"We're going to have to climb over those rocks," Harley finally said, pointing downward.

TJ had become unusually quiet. As they eased their way over a final huge stone, TJ cleared his throat, trying to get Harley's attention. "It's really dark in there."

"Well, at least we can't get locked inside," Harley offered. He meant it as a joke, but TJ didn't laugh. "Look, TJ, if we just stick together, we'll be all right." They sat down next to each other, reaffirming their commitment. Harley dropped the pouch on the space between them. As he tilted the waterskin to his lips, TJ noticed that the owl figure on Harley's amulet blinked twice.

"Harley," he said anxiously, "the owl blinked—twice."

Harley pulled up the amulet. The creatures on both sides were stiff and lifeless. "Maybe I'm supposed to do something." They looked around. Nothing occurred to them until both boys zeroed in on the pouch. Harley opened it and pulled out the message. "Look, TJ," he said excitedly, "there are more lines on it."

> Forlorn virgin youth will beg and cry.
>
> To peer again at Apollo's sky.
>
> Ignore them—leave not the righteous path.
>
> You want not to stir the Minotaur's wrath.
>
> Human flesh and their blood yet he craves.
>
> Make not his home your ultimate graves.
>
> Light a torch marking the way below.
>
> Keep wits alert—search both high and low.

Harley folded the parchment and stuck it back in the pouch. "It's going to be dark in there."

"Harley," TJ finally spoke up, "if they are all already dead, how can they talk to us?"

"I don't think it really matters, TJ," Harley answered. "The message said we have to ignore them."

"What if I mess up down there, Harley?" TJ confessed. "You know how I feel about dark places and ghosts."

"TJ," Harley continued, "we don't believe in ghosts—do we?" TJ still looked worried. "The Minotaur and those poor Athenians—well, they're long gone—if you know what I mean."

TJ knew exactly what his friend meant. However, he felt fuzzy and this whole experience was far from normal. The message said that the monster still craved flesh and blood. What did that mean?

Harley studied his friend's nervous reaction. He had to devise a way to keep TJ out of the maze while he searched for the bloody ball of string.

CHAPTER 18

SPLITTING UP

"I've been thinking, TJ," Harley began, "if both of us go down into the Labyrinth, we could both become lost and neither of us find our way out." He paused, letting his idea sink in. "I'm thinking that if one of us stays here by the only way out, he can make noises, so whoever is inside can hear his way out. What do you think?"

TJ bristled. "Harley, I'm not afraid to go in there."

"Didn't say you were," defended Harley. "I'm just thinking about the best way to do this. Ms. Clio said that the maze is massive and very confusing."

"Well, just so you know," insisted TJ, "I'm not afraid."

"Here's how I see it," Harley went on, ignoring TJ's remark, "you can whistle and I can't. So you stay here and I'll go inside. As long as I can hear you, I'll be able to find my way back."

"I can do that," TJ agreed, "whistle, that is. There's one more thing we have to remember. Ms. Clio said that time is fluid, especially when anyone crosses into a different dimension of time and space—like we did."

"Okay, but I don't feel any different."

Harley still had not seen or felt the undulating air waves that seemed to surround the area. He did recall that time was layered, and that depending on how the wind blew and the disruption of ever-moving clouds, time and space could fluctuate. Probably he and TJ were stirring the air by just being there. Together they inched their way downward to the actual opening in total silence.

"Harley!"

"What?"

"Harley, what if time changes back to the reality of the past and the Minotaur becomes real?"

Harley didn't answer right away. He had worried about the same thing, too. "We just have to do the best we can, TJ. That's just how it has to be." They kept moving forward and downward. Only a sliver of the bright Cretan sky peeked over the tops of the rubble of boulders above them.

"Wish I had a flashlight," Harley said, staring into the abyss.

"Let's make a torch," TJ suggested. He immediately began searching for something to burn. The remnants of an ancient torch lay off to the right. He raced to the spot and found dried grass blades to twist around it. "How's this?" he asked. "Now we just need a way to fire it up."

A crow cawed hoarsely in the distance. Harley grabbed his amulet. Do you think if we strike this metal against one of those stones we can start a fire?"

"We can try it," TJ agreed, "but let's make sure no breeze can blow it out."

They arranged a pile of very fine and extremely dry blades of dead grass. Harley found a stone about the size of his hand and placed it next to the pile. He lifted his amulet from his neck. "This is metal." He struggled to find the perfect angle to glance the blow of the metal edge against the hard stone before he actually saw a spark. "Look, TJ, it works." He struck harder with regular blows until the tiny sparks danced about the grassy kindling. It caught—a tiny plume of smoke began to wriggle upward. "Blow softly on it."

As TJ blew lightly into the smoke, a snapping sound grew from the pile. "We did it," he laughed. "We made fire."

They dipped the revamped torch into the flames; it caught immediately and burned brightly. "This ought to do it," Harley said with finality. "It's time for me to go inside." He rose abruptly, leaving his friend to put out the small fire. "Okay, TJ," he called back, "whistle every few minutes so I can get my bearings."

TJ stood up to watch his best friend in the world walk straight into danger. "Okay, Harley," he agreed, "but you be really, really careful. Don't do anything stupid."

Harley laughed. "Do I ever?"

"Yeah, sometimes you DO do stupid things, Harley," TJ laughed back at him. "I'll keep whistling. Find me, Harley."

"Got it."

"One more thing, Harley, keep your back to the wall and don't be taken in by those things—they're not real."

"That's two things, TJ."

Harley secretly hoped that the only real things he would encounter in the maze were lizards, bats, and maybe a few bugs. Those things he could handle; ghostly spirits were another story.

"You're the bravest kid I know," TJ called after him, but Harley didn't hear him. The crow cawed again almost mocking him. Harley was out of sight and TJ was alone. "Whistle," he scolded himself. "Whistle!"

TJ whistled a variety of shrill chirps as if he were calling birds. No birds came. Then he tried re-forming his mouth and lips to make louder sounds that varied in pitch. TJ was sure that the shadows around him had stretched even closer. He shivered, not from the cold, but rather from the piercing chill that had gripped his chest deep down inside.

He had a habit of imagining all the "what ifs" of a situation. Harley once told him that he was born an old man. He definitely lacked the daredevil exuberance of his best friend. His head ached. "What if Harley gets hurt?" and "What if he can't find his way out?" and "What if the monster finds him and eats him?" and "What if he can't find the artifact?" His young heart beat faster. He decided to whistle harder.

This time he belted the theme from TVLAND's *Bonanza*. It was good tune. It made him focus on all the notes. The "what ifs" faded into the background.

In another world a dog began to bark eagerly. Apollo lay with his nose against the chalkline circle.

"What's wrong, Apollo?" Tamiko asked.

"He's just missing the boys," Azlynn explained.

In truth Apollo heard the whistling. He easily identified TJ. He waited to hear his boy call his name, but Harley didn't call him. Apollo lay back down. He would wait for his boys to come home. He whimpered as if holding back a hard cry. He would wait to the end.

"Good boy," Tamiko said, patting his haunches. "They know you're worried and waiting for them to come home."

Apollo's ears perked up. He could hear familiar notes from a faraway place: "Who Let the Dogs Out?"

"Woof!"

CHAPTER 19

LABYRINTH

Only a few feet into the cavern, Harley felt a prickly chill creep up his spine. He shook it off and kept moving. With his feet firmly planted, Harley made a 180º visual survey of the entrance to the Labyrinth. He had traded his grass torch for an oil-based torch he found inside the structure. Now he could see six separate passageways. "Where should I start?" he asked the braver Harley inside his head.

When Ms. Clio shared the myth of the great and clever Athenian, she reminded the class that no man knows the depth of his own courage until he is faced with his greatest fear. And so it was with Theseus, who actually volunteered to enter the maze for the sole of killing the beast. Harley doubted that Theseus was ever really afraid of anything. After all, he fought the massive beast bare-handed.

Early in life Harley discovered the one thing that scared him the most—being alone. When his dad died and his mother checked out, Harley was alone and he was scared. Apollo, not much more than a great big puppy, saved him.

His security at this very moment was that Apollo, TJ, and the girls were waiting for him. He wasn't alone and he wasn't scared.

Somewhere behind him, he heard the theme song from his and TJ's favorite Western—*Bonanza*. The notes were familiar and reassuring. He scanned the area looking for a sign of some sort that might direct his next step. Even though Theseus was directed to reroll the ball of thread to retrace his route out, he didn't do that. So, as far as Harley could discern, the trail of that ball of thread still existed.

"If I can find that first post where Theseus attached the end of the thread, then I can begin to follow the trail."

Deeper inside about ten feet from the entrance, Harley spotted a splintered pole of wood. He tipped his torch closer and angled it in several directions for a better view. "Aha!" he breathed a sign of relief. A frail, two-inch length of cord peeked out from a pile of rock and wood. "This has to be it." Harley reached to pull at the cord, but to his dismay, it nearly crumbled to dust at his touch.

"One thing's for sure," he decided, "I'm not going to be able to hold on to it to follow it." He turned toward the nearest dark hole that yawned into the maze. "I'll have to stay low to the ground so I can see what's left of the string as I work my way to the center.

Just then a whistling rendition of "Who Let the Dogs Out?" drifted into the cavern. TJ, Harley's anchor, was still on duty at the entrance. Harley smiled. The shrill notes rallied his spirit. "Here goes nothing," he said, pushing the torch ahead of every step.

Perilous piles of jagged stones and a horrible stench of decay slowed his progress. The tunnel felt timeless, without substance. Harley couldn't tell if he had traversed 50 feet or 50 yards. Despite the flickering illumination from his torch, the blackness around him seemed all-consuming. Every few steps, Harley searched for evidence of the twine. It made him think of the safety harnesses used by acrobats. Even if they were to fall in the middle of a performance, someone at the other end could pull them back to safety. This place felt like a dream—no, it felt like a nightmare.

Harley inched his way along the wall, sometimes brushing his hand through cobwebs and dried, packed globs of mud that seemed to have dripped down the walls. That smell! Harley wrinkled his nose at the putrid odor of dampness and decay. The stench of sewer was growing stronger the deeper into the tunnel he traveled.

Luckily, every time he had to choose between openings in the maze, he was able to find evidence of Theseus's lifeline.

A strange sound emanating from deeper inside the tunnel drew his attention. He wasn't alone, and TJ was way back behind. Harley realized he hadn't heard his whistle for some time.

A frightened flutter of bats raced past him headed down the length of the tunnel he had just traveled. Harley froze; his torch flickered wildly in the rush of air. He felt the temperature drop; he could almost see his breath.

Coming toward him swirled an iridescent funnel of air that seemed to bounce off the walls of the passageway. Harley watched in fascination. It wasn't just air; it seemed to take form—the shape of a young woman dressed in a gossamer gown of light that trailed behind her. Actually, her presence was more awe-inspiring than frightening.

The girl was made of light and air. Yet Harley could easily make out her face and her reaching arms. Her hair danced wildly around her head, like the way Harley had pictured Medusa's serpents. The girl twirled and swirled around in endless pursuit of something.

"Who are you?" Harley dared to ask.

The figure stopped suddenly, trying to locate the position of the ruffled air. She had no real eyes—only dark holes. She twisted and turned until she floated within inches of Harley's shaking hands. Her bluish white trail of gown and hair wrapped protectively around her body. She seemed to be studying Harley.

"I'm Harley."

The form expanded and shivered violently. Harley was sure she was frightened of something.

Her face suddenly contorted into a grotesque mask of fear. Though Harley couldn't understand Greek, he understood exactly what her empty mouth was screaming at him. The light spirit beat her chest and pulled at her tangled locks and repeated her plea, "Save me!"

Though she was begging for Harley's help, she wasn't real. She was wind and light, but she exuded a powerful sense of desperation and fear.

"I'd like to help," Harley said to the form, which immediately doubled over into a glowing ball of pulsating blue light, "but I'm on a quest and…" The girl made of light stretched her form into a long, narrow beam, trying to disappear, "and I can't leave this path."

The female form shook angrily. Harley continued, "See, I'm following Theseus's thread to the center. "He pointed to a length of cord trapped between two slabs of cementlike stone. "I've got to find the ball of thread.

The form seemed to listen and to understand. She began racing back and forth in a frenzy. Then he heard it. Another sound, deeper and more menacing, thundered outward from the bowels of the maze. The spirit form froze. Two more gusts of wind-bodies rushed past. In their desperation to get away, they flew into each other, entwining their shimmering forms and then pulling apart over and over, as if unsure what to do or where to go.

Harley turned to the glowing girl before him and shouted, "What's wrong?"

She flew into her companions, twisting in and out of their light before returning to Harley. She clearly formed a word that Harley knew well. Though no sound escaped her throat, Harley knew exactly what she was screaming.

"RUN!"

CHAPTER 20

TESTING THE WATERS

THE CONSTANT WHISTLING LEFT TJ's throat parched. He remembered a rivulet about 50 yards from the Labyrinth. The water bag Epimenides had given them was dry. TJ needed to refill it, not only for himself, but he knew that Harley would also be thirsty when he returned.

It would take him no more than five minutes to get to the stream, fill the bag, and return to his post. He rationalized that if he couldn't whistle loud enough, Harley might not be able to hear him and find his way out. On the other hand, if Harley yelled for him while he was away from his post, he would not hear his voice—then what?

In the end, thirst won out. TJ climbed expertly up, over, and around the boulders and wood chunks. He then raced across the knoll toward the stream. All the while, he repeated, "Be okay, Harley, I'll be right back."

In some places the stream was no more than a foot wide. He studied its path bubbling over smooth stones. It looked clean; it smelled pure. He cupped his hand and drew a mouthful to his lips. He drank and waited. Nothing happened…no growling intestines…no upchucking…no cramps. Quickly he slipped the bag below the surface. A tiny brook trout wriggled past his hand and then it wasn't a trout. It became a lovely young woman… no, a little girl. Her faced aged and renewed its youth right before his eyes.

The youthful face looked deeply at TJ. "Hello," she gurgled. "Who are you?"

TJ attempted to rise and pull the bag from the water, but she held him tightly in her grip. "Let me go, please," he begged. "I have to get back."

"Who are you?" the naiad asked again.

"I am TJ Harris."

She repeated his words, "TJ Harris." Then she giggled and a gush of tiny bubbles popped to the surface. "You make beautiful music."

"Music?"

"Yes, your sound dances over my home and pleases me immensely." Her tone changed slightly. "I want you to come home with me so I can hear your music all the time."

TJ yanked his arm backward again but to no avail. The water sprite was stronger than a child. The determined look on her face told him that she was serious and probably dangerous. He had to think of a way to appease her.

"You liked my whistling?" he asked.

"Whistling," she mimicked. "That sounds like the work of the wind."

"You are clever, my water friend," said TJ. "That's exactly what it is—wind." He sat more comfortably on the bank of her stream. Her grip loosened only slightly. "You know," he went on with his plan, "I can make whistle music just for you and teach you how to do it yourself."

"Just for me," she tittered, "a whistle song—my song." Her watery gaze seemed to drift away from her focus on him. "Show me," she insisted.

"You will have to let me go so I can get what I need to show you," he said, pulling at his trapped arm.

She tightened her grip. TJ winced. "You can trust me," he promised. "Like the priestess at Delphi, I speak only the truth."

"She's a crazy one," the naiad laughed. "She sits above vapors and speaks of the future...Apollo's servant." Yet, the naiad believed and released her grip.

TJ combed through rich, green grass along the shore looking for a perfect blade. He found it and plucked it close to the ground. Gently, he brushed away the grit and returned to the naiad. "Watch and listen," he said.

He pinched the blade between his forefinger and thumb. Carefully, he stretched it to the ball of flesh below his thumb. Next, he used his ring finger to hold the blade of grass flatly, but firmly, in place. He showed her how to press the ball below the thumb of his other hand against the same place his ring finger had secured. The thin blade was held in place. Now he touched his fingers to each other as if praying. The sprite, who had joined him on the bank, watched and imitated every step. His thumbs held the grass while he pressed his lips to the opening and blew over the taut blade. A beautiful tone rang across the stream. The little naiad did the same.

TJ adjusted the flow of air and the narrowness of his lips to change the notes. She was thrilled. This was her whistle...her song, and she loved it. "You will not have to stay with me," she told him, "for I have your music and my very own whistle song." With that, she dived below the surface and swam away like a shimmering brook trout.

Desperate to return, TJ grabbed the full water bag and raced back to the entrance. Nothing there had changed—but he had changed. The touch of the water nymph seemed to have refreshed his spirit. In fact, he felt unusually strong and full of energy. Once again he began to whistle. This time the sounds he made filled the cavern with hope.

For a few moments, Harley thought he heard the cheerful melody of the Mickey Mouse Club. The notes were crisp as TJ sent out his clarion call. More pressing matters redirected his attention. He was standing his ground, but his knees were shaking. If these spirit people were afraid of something that was coming through the maze, then it would be wise of him to also be afraid. The Minotaur of the Labyrinth had begun his rampage.

The ground began to shake more fiercely. Harley was momentarily confused. The tiny pebbles around his feet began to dance like Mexican jumping beans on fire.

"Holy cow," Harley muttered. "This is no spirit happening; this is real."

He searched the rubble for a place to hide. The stench of the Labyrinth grew more intense. And then he heard it. The bellowing of the unseen beast …louder and louder. Harley was right in its path. He couldn't risk the monster spotting his torch, so he shoved it into a crevice where it nearly extinguished itself. Only a tiny tendril of flame remained aglow.

The roar grew louder; Harley pulled back into his hiding place even deeper. Between bellows of the beast, Harley heard a dog barking. "TJ and Apollo," he whispered. "I am not alone." And then the beast blew into the passageway. It stopped before him.

The Minotaur paused at this intersection, sniffing the air in hopes of capturing the scent of his prey. It rose to its full ten feet. From the chest to the top of its horned head, it was a snarling, ravenous killer—a bull. Its massive, muscular lower body was that of a powerful man. It roared angrily, spewing a putrid layer of spittle foam on the surrounding walls. Unlike the glowing light surrounding the humanoid spirits who came before it, this creature was shrouded in a cloud of murky, gray, smoke-filled air.

It turned its head in Harley's direction, sniffing deeply. Then it sniffed again as if it had detected something—something alive. It stepped even closer and leaned into the rocks that barely concealed Harley. The boy didn't move a muscle; he didn't even blink. The Minotaur was looking right at him, but Harley realized that it couldn't see him.

Harley looked deep inside the beast's eyeholes. He not only saw, but also felt, the heat of the molten lava of a threatening volcano. The cloud that roiled in turmoil about the beast began to infuse itself into the Minotaur's body, turning it into nothing but a ball of fetid air and blackness. It turned and thundered off in the direction the Athenian spirits had taken only minutes ago. Harley was alone again in this ancient tomb.

Whew! Harley let out the huge breath he'd been holding. "That was close," he sighed. He pulled his torch from the fissure and coaxed it into a brilliant flame. "I've got to find that ball of thread and get out of this place."

The deeper into the maze he ventured, the more gruesome the debris. He saw the mangled fur of animal carcasses and the tangled bones of all kinds of creatures. He walked on and on; he lost all sense of time. Harley's perception of this experience blended the reality of his senses with the fantasy of his imagination. Someone had actually built this place. Was there really a monster living down here? Had he actually seen and heard and smelled the Minotaur? Harley brushed these questions aside. He had a task to complete; Sammy was depending on him.

He shuddered. There was a change in the air. Ahead of him there must be a void; he felt as if the passage had narrowed. Now the atmosphere felt electric, tense, and foreboding. He knew not what awaited him, but still, he knew what he must do.

Chapter 21

The Beast

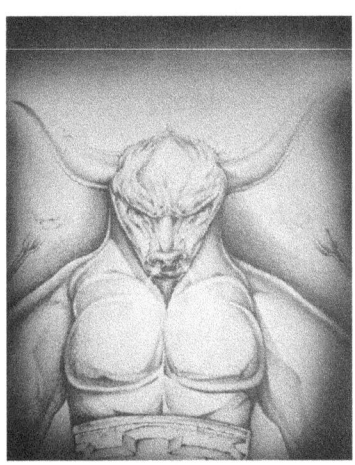

The main cavern of the Labyrinth was huge. Sections of the ceiling stones had collapsed, littering the floor below. Harley tested his footing as he crossed over each massive block. Despite his determined effort to find the ball of thread, he couldn't see it anywhere. Perhaps it lay buried beneath one of the huge stone slabs.

"Maybe I missed something," he said. "This time I'll mark the sections I've already searched." He mentally divided the hall into quadrants. As he completed his search of one quadrant, he planned to scratch an X into the earth as a reminder. However, he decided to construct a pylon of stones to mark the mouth of the tunnel from which he had emerged. "That's the way back to TJ," he said.

He brushed the rock dust from his hands and grabbed the torch that he had wedged between two solid stones. As before, he stretched his arm to cast the torch's light into every nook and cranny. The air so far below the surface should have been cool, but it was hot and humid. After searching almost three-fourths of the room, Harley's skin was bathed in sticky sweat. He was becoming dehydrated. He knew that if he didn't find the artifact soon, he might never make his way back. The last thing he wanted was for TJ to come down into the maze looking for him.

Harley looked up from his search. The glow in the cavern hall seemed to have doubled in lumens. His torch, small as it was, had not changed. Yet he could now see, quite clearly, the entire room—from wall to wall. A fiery indigo tint emanated from the passageway opposite Harley's location. "What in the world...?"

Instead of the bluish, electric, diaphanous aura of the Athenian spirits, this projection seemed to be bathed in a regal blaze of a commanding bluish-red hue. It was more solid than the others and exuded a sense of power. As it emerged in its entirety, the room began to glow brilliantly. Harley could see everything in the room as clear as if it were high noon back home.

The purplish orb materialized before him. Unlike the blue spirits, this one was confident, unafraid. It pulsated intensely, as if waiting for something to happen.

"Hello," Harley stuttered. "I'm Harley Delosian. Who are you?"

The orb turned toward him. It began to swell in size. It took the shape of a person, the mass quivering as if in satisfaction that it had found what it was looking for. Its glow burned even hotter—Harley stepped back; it was almost a white fire.

"Are you..." Harley dared to ask, "are you Theseus?"

The white glow began to dim to violet, then purple flame, before resuming its original indigo light. Vibrant purple sparks periodically shot through his body.

He was a young man with long dark hair that seemed to conduct the static electricity that surged throughout his nearly translucent form. His stance was that of a magnificent warrior.

"You are Theseus," Harley decided aloud.

The vision beat his right hand against his chest. He mouthed the unmistakable words, "I am Theseus, the son of King Aegeus and the future King of Athens."

"I'm Harley, and I'm from another time."

The spirit dimmed slightly and leaned in closer to the boy to get a better look.

"I know who you are," Harley said proudly. "I've read about you in school." Theseus seemed to want to know more; Harley continued, "I'm looking for that ball of thread you left behind down here."

The glowing man-spirit spiraled around Harley as if judging his worth. When he stopped swirling and faced Harley, the boy decided to speak again. "Can you help me find the..." He stopped midsentence. The atmosphere in the cavern had suddenly changed.

An ominous rumbling sounded from deep inside one of the passageways that emptied in the center where Harley and the Theseus spirit stood. The monster was coming. A red glow grew in intensity. Harley took it as a warning and searched for a place to hide.

This time Harley forgot his torch. It stood between two stones and continued to burn weakly out in the open. "Please don't go out," he pled.

The Theseus form began to change. The violet energy was evolving into a purple-black glow with throbbing red edges. Each time Theseus pounded his chest, a burst of blue-indigo exploded inside his body. Theseus pointed to two large slabs of ceiling rock that had fallen on top of each other. Harley recognized it as a perfect hiding place.

So far, he realized that it was sound that drew these spirits to him. Tucked tightly among the rocks, Harley was determined to be as quiet as a mouse—no matter what happened in the center arena.

The black cloud of the Minotaur burst through the tunnel and stopped at the sight of Theseus. It seemed to clearly recognize its enemy. The beast snorted volcanic red through its nostrils and bellowed its challenge. Harley curled up even smaller in his hiding place, but could not tear his eyes away from the scene in the center. Mythic history was unfolding before him.

Then—it happened. The air around him seemed to ripple. Something else was going on. The room no longer pulsated, but rather it flickered in torchlight. The ghostly form of Theseus was now a man, a real man, clad in a wraparound loincloth. The Minotaur, too, had transformed into all of its horrific, solid glory. Like wrestlers, the two squared off and began circling each other, looking for the perfect opportunity to engage.

The Minotaur howled in fury. Hungry for Athenian blood, it charged Theseus. Because the monster was filled with rage, it was no match for the battle-trained warrior. Theseus was quick and evaded the Minotaur's grasp. He danced around the monster like Ali would in the modern boxing ring. The monster became confused, which fueled its anger even more.

Theseus positioned himself to successfully grapple with the beast. His superiority at hand to hand combat allowed him to easily maneuver the monster into a weaker position. Theseus locked on. The Minotaur tried to pull away, but Theseus held firmly. Next, he used the element of surprise to sweep the beast's footing, causing both of them to fall to the floor. Theseus wrapped both his legs around the beast's torso. He began pounding its ribcage with unrelenting strength. The Minotaur wailed in agony.

Harley knew the outcome of their battle. He didn't know if he could watch it. And then, the air rippled again. The flickering torches faded into the phantasmic glow of the mythological beings at center stage. The brilliantly purple Athenian jumped off the back of the smoky black form of the Minotaur.

Theseus pounded his chest in victory. The Minotaur inhaled all its scattered cloud and dashed down the nearest tunnel. Harley thought he could hear its howl fade as it escaped the Athenian. Theseus's battle glow began to dim into a warmer aura.

Harley crawled out from among the slabs of stone. His heart beat so hard that he was sure Theseus could hear it. "That was the most amazing thing I have ever seen in my life," Harley said to the Athenian hero. "I think I understand what happened." The warrior nodded in approval.

Theseus strode over to a pile of heavy stones. He thrust his glowing arm deep inside the spaces and withdrew a bloody ball of thread. He turned to Harley and pointed to his leather pouch. Harley opened the pouch and Theseus lowered the ball inside. Through indigo holes for eyes, Theseus looked into Harley's soul and nodded his approval once again. His work was done. He pulled himself into a vibrating orb of brilliant light and shot away into a tunnel.

Harley just stood there and watched. He was so awestruck that he could say nothing until the orb had disappeared. "Thank you," he said in a voice barely audible. "Thank you."

The melodic notes of "99 Bottles of Beer" filtered into the cavern. "TJ."

Harley grabbed his torch and turned in the direction of his rock pylon marker. His journey back to the surface was uneventful. This task of the journey was complete. He saw the light of the Cretan sky ahead. TJ's whistling was a welcoming beacon.

"TJ!" Harley yelled. "I did it! I've got the ball of thread in the pouch!"

"Harley," TJ cried happily. "You're safe…you're back…you look different."

CHAPTER 22

Water

TJ had never felt as relieved as he did at this moment. Harley had come back in one piece. He had the spool of bloody thread tucked safely inside the pouch. On the other hand, TJ noticed a subtle change in Harley. It was as if he were no longer the carefree kid from the cul-de-sac.

"I'm really hot and sweaty," Harley told his friend as they walked away from the maze. With each step, the air around the Labyrinth rippled. The Cretan sun blazed high in the sky. "I thought it would be later than that," Harley said, pointing at the position of the sun.

"There's a stream just over there," TJ said. He worried that Harley might encounter the naiad as well, so added, "Why don't we move upstream before we figure out where to go next."

"Sounds like a good idea to me," Harley agreed. "By the way, I could hear you whistling, and it really helped. How was it for you out here?"

"It was okay," TJ said, telling a half-truth. "I had to leave for a few minutes to fill the water bag."

They reached the bank of the stream where a pool had formed. Tall reeds reached above the surface, inviting Harley to take a dip. "I'm going to wash the cave grime off my body," Harley announced. He stepped into a grove of bushes and stripped down, then tiptoed into the welcoming cool water.

TJ surveyed the water. The naiad was nowhere to be seen. Harley should be okay. "Hurry up, Harley, we've got more to do."

Harley sank into the pool. The reeds surrounding him seemed to buzz excitedly. "Stranger, stranger," Harley thought he heard whispering. "Stranger among us. Stranger among us."

TJ also heard the whispering. He realized that the reeds were moving closer to Harley as if they were trying to imprison him. "Harley!" TJ shouted, "get out of there!" Harley was in a daze; he neither saw what was happening nor heard the reeds' murmuring any longer. TJ tried to run through the water to pull Harley out of danger, but his feet were cemented to the ground. He needed help.

TJ reached for a green blade of grass and positioned it perfectly. He blew threw his thumbs and a shrill whistle wafted across the water. Nothing. He did it again and again. The beautiful shimmer of a rainbow trout appeared among the mossy stones underwater. It swam right up to TJ and rose from the water in the form of a very young woman.

"My song," it said sweetly. "You whistled my song."

"I did," TJ said urgently. "Those water plants are trying to pull my friend underwater. He can't hear me and I can't move." He looked at the vision with pleading eyes. "Can you help him?"

The water sprite looked toward the reeds. A naked boy was being covered with layers of reeds. "They are calling him a stranger and they are trying to protect themselves."

"He's not a stranger," TJ pleaded. "He's my best friend and we're on a quest to save the life of another friend."

"You and he are of the same world—the same place?"

"Yes, we are. He's just like me."

The naiad thought of TJ as her friend; therefore, the naked boy, no matter his oddness, must also be a friend. "I'll talk with them." She returned to fish form and swam among the reeds. The buzz was amplified as if they were arguing. Then, everything was quiet.

One by one, the reeds began to rise up, releasing their grip. Harley shook his head and realized he had cooled off enough. He stood in the water and stepped back into the bushes to dress, then joined TJ on the bank. "Is there anything left to eat?" He seemed to have no memory of his close call.

Again they snacked on cheese and flat bread. "What do we do now?" TJ asked. A crow cawed in the distance. The owl on Harley's amulet blinked.

"I think we have a new message," Harley said as he reached inside the pouch for the parchment. He unrolled it slowly; both boys watched the ancient script translate into a language they could decipher:

> To Thessaly you must find your way.
>
> Hear what Mother Justice has to say.
>
> Challenge Lachesis to add the thread.
>
> To extend the life of the boy in the bed.

"Thessaly," TJ sighed. "That's on the mainland of Greece. How do we get there?"

Harley pondered the problem. "We could follow this stream to the coast and try to catch a ship."

"That would take too long."

"Okay, TJ," he conceded. "What do you suggest?"

"Well, think about it, Harley," he began. "How did we get here? Couldn't we use that to get us somewhere else?"

"But the girls aren't here," Harley reminded him. "What if we find ourselves back home instead of in Thessaly?"

Harley made a good point. "Let's try it anyway. We can use the amulets in place of Tamiko and Azlynn and still form a circle." So they did.

They sat facing each other with the leather cord of the amulets connecting them. Each boy held his own amulet in his right hand. "Let's concentrate...maybe we should close our eyes," TJ suggested. The air around them slowly began to undulate. The tiny ripples grew into waves—bigger and bigger waves of air until the boys rocked like ocean flotsam. "Don't open your eyes, TJ, until everything stops moving." The amulets glowed brilliantly in the sunshine. And then it stopped.

Harley dared a peek. He breathed deeply. The air felt different. It wasn't as moist as it had been. They had done it. They were no longer on Crete, but somewhere else, hopefully Thessaly.

"TJ," he called, "open your eyes."

TJ complied. When he opened his eyes, a whole new terrain lay before him. In the distance was the tallest mountain he had ever seen. It was so tall that a thick ring of cloud mist hid its peak from view.

"Mount Olympus," he uttered in amazement. "We did it."

The great mountain stood 9570 feet, or 2917 meters high, according to what TJ remembered from class. It was magnificent. A forest blocked human access. Jagged stones littered the areas that were bare of trees, high above the timberline.

"In those clouds," TJ said, "is hidden the gate to the palace of the Olympians. It's guarded by the Seasons, protective spirits who drift freely inside the cloud, allowing no mortal to enter."

"We're mortals," Harley reminded his friend.

Nevertheless, they turned toward it and began climbing the massive giant. The trek was slow and perilous. They could hear the constant nagging of a crow. It seemed to be taunting them: "Caw, you can't do this. Caw, it's too high. Caw, go back." They ignored the bird and pulled themselves up the mountain, determined to prove it wrong. Harley and TJ were not alone. Far above, others were watching them.

"Certainly they've proven themselves by now," Apollo said to his father. "Can you not allow them even a short hearing?"

"They are her mortals," Zeus thundered, alluding to the Muse Clio.

"Yes, and Clio has pleaded their case before deaf ears."

"What would you have us do?" asked Hera.

"All they want is to present their case to Themis, the judge of all that is right. All I am asking is to hear what they have to say. Let her weigh their plea and determine the outcome."

"They cannot pass through the gates without an offering to place at the feet of Justice," Zeus ordered.

"What kind of offering would appease the great Mother of Law and Justice?" Athena asked.

The regal Titan studied the two young mortals for a moment before speaking. "They are like loyal brothers who would go to the ends of the earth to protect each other. From them I want a tear of mourning sisters who witnessed their brother fall out of the sky to his death…because a father called upon the Styx to seal a promise of folly."

"So it shall be done," Athena said as she faded into the mist.

Though they struggled for what seemed like hours, the boys realized that they had hardly made a dent in their climb.

"Harley, let's take a break," TJ suggested. They found a smooth, flat stone and climbed onto it. "I'm worried that this is going to take too long."

"Me, too," Harley said as he tilted the water bag to his parched lips. "I almost feel like someone or something is blocking our way." The familiar sound of the crow echoed in the distance. Harley raised his amulet to see if the owl blinked. It did. "We've got another message." He read the poetic stanza aloud:

> "Before Justice will hear your pleading
>
> Offer a tear of sisters mourning
>
> From the shallows of Eridanus
>
> A place where man has yet to witness."

TJ listened, trying to absorb the gravity of the message. "Harley," he finally said, "we have to go to a place where no human has ever gone. I don't know if it's a secret place or a forbidden place."

"Well, let's try to connect the dots," Harley decided. "No matter what, we have to do this."

They figured out that Eridanus must be a river off the beaten trail. "I don't know where this river is," admitted TJ. "How can we find a place we know nothing about?"

"What I don't get is that we're supposed to bring back a tear from this river," Harley said, scratching his head. "How do we separate a tear from river water?"

The owl blinked again. Athena was sending them another message. Harley saw the inked writing grow more lines. "Look!" he shouted, and they both leaned in to read:

> A father's promise sealed by the Styx.
>
> Condemns a witless youth with eyes fixt.
>
> On the chariot that brings the light.
>
> Scorching heaven and earth while in flight.

"Okay," TJ said, sitting up taller. "It's talking about that kid who almost destroyed the world."

CHAPTER 23

Tears

After TJ retold the story about Phaëton's ill-fated ride in his father's chariot, the boys once again used their amulet circle and transported themselves to an unknown location—the banks of the Eridanus. The river was unexpectedly wider than most of the streams they had encountered.

"I see how it was able to catch him," Harley said. "It must be pretty deep out there."

"The clue said that what we're looking for is in the shallow part of the river," TJ reminded his companion. "I vaguely remember that Helios, Phaëton's dad, also had daughters from a different mother. So, if they watched Phaëton fall out of the sky after he lost control of the horses pulling the chariot and Zeus struck him with a thunderbolt, then they must have been here when he hit the water."

"It's a river in both directions," Harley complained. "There's nothing but bushes and reeds growing everywhere."

"No, Harley," TJ said excitedly. "Look."

A copse of poplar trees had sprouted in an almost hidden glen. The tall, angular trees were wrapped in thin white bark striped haphazardly with ribbons of black. The tops swayed rhythmically in the gentle breeze.

"Don't they look like a group of very tall girls?" TJ asked.

"They look like trees, TJ," Harley answered, "but around here, nothing is what it seems." He threw his arm over TJ's shoulders and started for the trees. "Let's check it out."

"Who was that?" Tamiko asked.

"It was my mom," Azlynn said, sliding her cell phone back into her pocket. "She went to the hospital to visit with Mrs. Crabtree."

"Did she say how Sammy's doing?"

"She said that he's getting weaker," Azlynn sniffed through tears that threatened to fall. "Mom said Mrs. Crabtree is exhausted and very worried."

"I hope Harley and TJ finish the quest soon," Tamiko said. "I wish we could do more to help than just sit around here in the treehouse."

"I know what you mean."

The girls discussed why such things like this happen. They agreed that Sammy was a harmless soul who never hurt anyone in his life. It seemed unfair that he should be so sick that the doctors couldn't help him.

"It's a good thing that Sammy has us," Azlynn said.

"I sure hope so," added Tamiko.

Apollo sighed with a slight whimper. He wanted his boys to return. Dogs seemed to have keener senses than boys. Apollo could feel that no harm had come to them, but that even greater challenges awaited them—they weren't ready to come home to him yet.

"Poor doggy," Tamiko said, rubbing behind his ears. "You are the perfect example of loyalty."

"I don't think he's moved more than an inch from the circle," Azlynn noticed. "He has more patience than I have." She wiped the tears from her cheeks. "I've never been so scared."

"They could make a mistake that might take them in the wrong direction," Tamiko worried.

"I trust what Ms. Clio said about people on the other side who are there to guide them, and, I suppose, help them if they get into serious trouble."

"We all placed our trust in her," Tamiko steadfastly returned.

"Here we are," Harley said, looking around the unusual grove. The trees are pretty close to the water's edge."

"Let's look along the edge where it's shallow," suggested TJ. "Maybe something will make itself known to us."

The brilliant sun remained high in the sky. Harley thought about what it was like for Phaëton. "Why didn't he listen to his father warning him about the dangers of his request to drive the chariot of fire at sunrise?"

"I guess he wasn't much different than kids today," TJ surmised. "They don't really hear what their parents tell them."

"If my father were alive," Harley said, "I think I would listen to him." The photograph of Trooper Charlie Delosian, his son Harley, and a big puppy called Apollo appeared in Harley's mind. "I wonder what he would have been like…I mean…you know."

TJ was splashing through the water, looking below the surface for tears when a glint of something caught his eye. He stopped and waited until the surface returned to calm. "Harley," he said in a low tone. "Harley, I found something." TJ reached carefully into the riverbed and wrapped his fingers around a smooth, yellowish-gold stone. It shone like a gemstone through the crystal clear water. His heart beat rapidly. "Could it really be this easy?"

Harley waded into the shallows to see what TJ had discovered. He watched as TJ lifted the yellow gem from the water.

"Look, Harley," TJ exclaimed as he thrust the object in front of Harley's face. "It looks like amber."

In the same second, Harley watched the orb of amber melt into water and fall back into the shallows.

"What!" TJ shouted with disappointment. "Where'd it go?"

"Do it again," Harley ordered. "Find another one."

TJ found stone after stone, but once each one surfaced, it melted and was lost in the water. Frustrated, the boys couldn't figure out why it was happening.

"How are we ever going to get the amber offering to Mother Justice?" Harley asked. "Are you sure the amber stones at the bottom of the stream are the teardrops of Phaëton's sisters?"

"Yes, Azlynn read me a poem that talked about how sorrowfully they cried until Zeus took pity, turning their tears into amber and them into poplar trees."

"So," Harley determined, "that they could stand watch over their brother's final resting place."

"Yeah, that seems to be the gist of it." The amber orbs were real; they could easily feel the mass of each one, but only when their hands were under water. The riverbed was covered in amber drops.

"It seems that the Eridanus wants to keep these tearful orbs," Harley decided. "We only need one." He thought for a moment before concluding, "We almost have to take the river with us if we want to get the amber stone to Mother Justice."

"You're right, Harley," TJ laughed. "I have an idea."

CHAPTER 24

AN OFFERING

HARLEY AND TJ SAT beneath the poplar trees. They shared the final drops of water from their goatskin jug. The treetops swayed heavily above them, the leaves murmuring in the breeze.

"Do you hear them?" TJ asked.

"Who?"

"The sisters still moaning in sorrow for their lost brother."

Harley listened. The breeze fluttering the leaves actually sounded like women crying endlessly. "Maybe it's their tears that keep his spirit alive deep under the water of the Eridanus."

"You're beginning to sound like Ms. Clio," laughed TJ.

"You don't say, Fuzzy Head."

They both laughed like twelve-year-olds whose main concern was nothing more than the next soccer match. Only a short time ago, they were those boys. Now, they felt as though the weight of the world was on their shoulders instead of on those of the giant Atlas.

"Are you ready?" Harley asked, rising from the ground.

"Let's do it."

When their task was complete, the boys joined hands in their amulet circle, closed their eyes, and focused their thoughts on Mount Olympus. The air around them quivered, sending ripples high into the heavens.

"Father, look at them," pleaded Apollo. "They have done what you asked." He paused, waiting for the perfect moment to continue.

The great Zeus turned to his brilliant son. "They are mortals. We cannot allow mortals to enter Mount Olympus and then leave again. Since time immemorial, it has never been done."

Apollo looked to his sister-cousin Athena. She nodded. "If a man…or a god…neglects his promise, why should he be respected or honored among his peers?"

"Be careful, Apollo, you are treading on dangerous ground."

"Apollo speaks the truth, as ever, Father," Pallas Athena announced. "It was your gift to him, whether it pleases you or not."

Themis spoke, "The law requires that a man's…or a god's word must be honored. Let them approach and present their offering. The tears of the sun sisters cannot be drawn from the Eridanus. If they do not make this offering, it is only right that they be judged by you."

Zeus smiled. "Bring them forth, but complain ye not when these young mortals must face another trio of sister, the Moirae."

Harley and TJ felt the quivering air around them calm. "Are your eyes open, Harley?"

"Not yet," he answered. "I have a funny feeling that we're not in Kansas anymore," he grinned.

They found themselves seated in the middle of a massive, marble room. The grand scale of it was beyond anything either of them could have imagined. One by one, seated visions appeared before them.

"Harley," whispered TJ, "that's Hera, the Queen of the Gods."

"How do you know?"

"She's petting a peacock, her favorite bird, and that's Iris, the rainbow goddess who attends her."

"Who's that?"

"That, Harley, is Poseidon, Master of the Seas. He holds his powerful trident in his left hand so that his right hand is free to hold the reins of his "horses.""

They watched as the hall filled with curious royalty. Beautiful Aphrodite stood among the immortals next to her husband, the crippled Hephaestus. Hermes lowered himself on winged sandals and landed next to a brilliantly glowing orb that became a powerful young man, Phoebus Apollo. The final two immortals to materialize seemed to command everyone's total attention.

Themis, the ancient Goddess of Justice, took her place to the right of almighty Zeus, God of the Universe, King of Gods and Men. The entire room fell silent. All eyes were lowered in respect for their lord. "Immortals of Mount Olympus," Zeus began, "look upon these mortals who dare to think they can enter our hallowed halls." Everyone looked at Harley and TJ, who were still seated in their circle.

"Rise," ordered Zeus.

The boys stood before the King of the Heavens. Their legs felt weak, yet the air they breathed filled their lungs with such vigor they thought they might fly.

"You are not the first mortals to pass through our gates. But know this," Zeus thundered. "No mortal has ever left through those gates."

Harley looked toward Apollo, who nodded an okay to him. Apollo tilted his head, mutely suggesting the boys step up. Bravery overcame fear; Harley stepped forward boldly but respectfully, stopping at the foot of Zeus's throne.

"May I have your permission to speak, my lord?"

"Brazen child," Zeus shouted. "You dare speak before you are asked!"

"I apologize, my lord, but we are almost out of time to save our friend, so forgive me for not standing on protocol." He had heard those words on television and thought they fit the occasion.

Zeus beckoned Hephaestus to bring before him the giant hourglass. A thick layer of grains of sand already filled the bottom of the bowl. "You are correct in this knowledge. Time is its own force. Neither god nor man can stop these grains from falling."

"If I may, sir, we must find our way to the sisters of Fate before it is too late."

TJ could hardly believe how brave his friend had become. Was this the change he saw in Harley when he exited the Labyrinth? Harley was not only extremely brave and self-confident, he was also extraordinarily articulate.

Hera turned to Zeus. "No one can influence the Fates. How does this foolish boy think he can approach them? "I am not foolish, your highness," Harley addressed her. "I have...we have a quest to complete. It is a matter of life and death and time is of the essence."

"You wish to speak to my daughters," said Themis. "I am their protector. Without my permit, you will never stand before them."

TJ finally spoke out, "We have brought you an offering in hopes of proving our sincerity." He raised the goatskin water bag.

"What is this?" Themis laughed. "The fat skin of a goat?"

"It's more than that, my lady," added Harley. "Let my companion show you."

Themis waved TJ closer. He stood at her feet. She, too, was a giant form emanating righteous power. TJ raised the goatskin bag to her.

"Feel gently on the outside. You will feel the solid mass of a stone, but not just any stone. Inside the sack lies a tear from mourning sisters. In the light of day it shines like the sun of Helios, but it cannot leave its watery home."

Themis opened the drawstring of the water bag. She peered inside. Still glowing, the amber gemstone beckoned her to lift it from its watery casing.

"You have done the impossible," Themis judged. "You have brought the Eridanus here inside this bag so that it could continue to protect the tear." She turned to the crowd of onlookers. They were eager to see the stone.

Themis poured the water onto the floor at her feet. As it filtered through her fingers, she caught the amber tear, stopping it from falling onto the floor.

"Ah," the immortals sighed, "the tears of the Heliades, sad daughters of Helios."

Just as quickly as it had done with the boys down in the shallows of the river, it melted and flowed through her fingers, joining the puddles on the floor.

"You have done well, young mortals; I will hear your case."

CHAPTER 25

"Hear Ye, Hear Ye"

The grand marbled room dissolved into a kind of courtroom. Themis sat at the head, holding her scales firmly. She, too, had shrunk in size, but not in power. The others sat in regal seats along both walls to the left and right of the boys. Zeus and Hera rose to a gallery loft that hovered above the entire space. They would watch with special interest.

"You may choose from among our Olympian family, not to include Zeus or Hera, those who will act as your advisors in these proceedings should you have questions about what is permissible."

Harley and TJ put their heads together to decide who they should invite to sit with them. "Apollo gave me a signal to step forward," Harley offered.

"That may be true," TJ said, but Athena is the Goddess of Wisdom and she is the favored child of Zeus."

"But Zeus is not going to decide our case; Themis is."

"I get your point." Harley didn't know who would best advise them. They were all with tremendous influence and insight. What they needed was one who could give them procedural advice while also appreciating their quest.

"What about him?" Harley asked, pointing in the direction of the beautiful Aphrodite.

"Hephaestus? Why him?"

"He is responsible for the beauty and splendor of this magnificent palace. They all respect his craft and, therefore, him as well. He is crippled and not as handsome as the others. He knows what it's like to be different."

"Oh," TJ said. "I understand your strategy. Let's go for it."

"Your Royal Justice," Harley announced, "we choose Hephaestus to join with us and advise us through these proceedings."

The crowd buzzed with surprise. The most obvious choices were Athena or Apollo, but these young mortals chose the blacksmith, of all gods, the one who works with his hands and cares nothing for politics. This hearing was proving to be interesting.

"Your choice is accepted," Themis pronounced. "Now present your claim so that I can decide who else must be called before me."

TJ patted Harley's back, encouraging him to tell everyone why they are there. "You can do this, Harley."

Harley stepped to the middle of the room, directly in front of the judge, Themis. He worried about where to begin his plea. He looked to Hephaestus.

"She wants to know why you have come here to ask a favor from the gods."

"Oh," Harley said. Now he knew exactly what to say. "My name is Harley Delosian, son of Charlie and Valoria Delosian." The crowd murmured. "My friend here," he pointed at TJ, "is TJ or Thomas Jarrell Harris, son of Jason and Lydia Harris." Again the murmur traveled the room.

"We are here to ask permission to speak with Lachesis of the Fates on behalf of our sick friend back home."

"How might the sister who weaves the life fabric of the living be of assistance to your friend?" Themis asked sternly.

"Tell her about the thread," Hephaestus suggested.

"I have in this pouch the ball of thread that the heroic Theseus left behind in the miserable Labyrinth of Crete. I want to ask Lachesis to weave the thread into the life tapestry of Samuel Crabtree, son of Niobe Crabtree."

"So, why do you come here first?" Themis demanded. "Would it not better serve your needs to go directly to the Moirae?"

"We know not where to find the three sisters," Harley explained. "Our teacher told us about the Fates and that they are not accessible nor influences by gods or men." The crowd nodded in agreement. "We are asking for an audience with Lachesis, something only you can arrange."

"I can bid them to appear before me," Themis told them. "I will do this only if I believe your case to be worthy." One side of her scale lowered as if an invisible weight had been added. "Tell me," she said, leaning closer to Harley, "why should Samuel Crabtree's life be lengthened?"

"Sammy…I mean Samuel…is one of the kindest, most sincere and loving human beings who was ever born." Harley looked back at Hephaestus. The craftsman nodded to him.

TJ had explained to the god how Sammy had fallen into a troubled sleep after hitting his head. He also explained Sammy's special gifts; he preferred not to call them needs. Hephaestus immediately identified with Sammy.

Harley continued, "Something has caused Sammy to remain sleeping. His doctor cannot find a cause or a cure. Once, when Sammy woke for a short while, he told me to follow Korvus. He told me to hurry."

The onlookers turned to Phoebus Apollo. Korvus was perched on his forearm. The black bird cawed sharply. Harley had become accustomed to its call. He realized that Korvus was never taunting them, but rather, he had been guiding them.

"If we can extend Sammy's life tapestry, then we will have more time to find the cure and get it to our friend."

"You have put your own lives in jeopardy so that your friend might live longer?"

"He is our friend," Harley explained. "There was no doubt in our minds that we had to complete this quest for Sammy. We never hesitated."

"You faced the Minotaur?"

"I did," Harley told the judge, "but it was not really interested in me. It was Theseus who fought him and he then showed me the ball of thread."

The crack of lightning and thunder sounded from outside the palace. The gods shuddered. A dark cloud wafted into the room. When it cleared, three old women stood before the august assembly.

"Daughters," insisted Themis, "you need not be so angry when you answer my call."

Clotho spoke first. "Mother, the time you call us here—no new life can be spun on my spindle."

"Without her thread," said Lachesis, "I cannot weave the life outcomes for those who live."

The most frightening of the trio raised her shears to the heavens. "I, on the other hand, can still cut the cord on those who think there is always a tomorrow. If I do this whilst they cannot fulfill their obligations, the race of mortals will only diminish."

"Then we shall complete these procedures with expediency," Themis said to the assembly. "As you can see, the scales of justice weigh heavily in favor of these young mortals. During your journey to these hallowed halls, you have heard their plea."

Lachesis stepped forward. "We have listened to their story. Never in all of history have we ever added thread to a life tapestry at the request of a mere mortal."

"Should we do this," Clotho said, "it would disrupt the balance of all life as we know it. Other mortals would beseech us to extend the lives of ones they love."

The scales began to change. The bowl opposite the weighted bowl representing Harley, TJ, and Hephaestus dropped, tilting the scale against them.

Harley jumped up. "But there is only one ball of thread such as the one we have. No other mortal will have access to it once we give it to you."

Harley's scale bowl dropped slightly.

"Mortal," Atropos addressed Harley, "what you have failed to learn is that the balance of life must never be trifled with. If we agree to extend the life of Samuel Crabtree, another life must be sheared earlier than originally spun out by Sister Lachesis."

Harley looked back at TJ, who shrugged helplessly. The countenance of Hephaestus drooped with heavy sadness. He, too, had forgotten this rule of the universe.

Harley cleared his throat so that he would be clearly understood. "Divine Mother of Justice, I freely and gladly give a measure of the thread of my life tapestry so that the thread that feeds the fabric of my friend Sammy may be extended."

"Ohh," the crowd exhaled.

"I do the same," shouted TJ. "You can take what you need from my life thread as well!"

Again, the onlookers gasped in unison.

"Why would you do this?" asked Lachesis. "Are not your lives good and wholesome?"

"Our lives are good," Harley explained, "and so is Sammy's life. He is loved by so many. He deserves a chance to live—just as we do."

The Moirae gathered. While they argued amongst themselves, their forms grew younger and more appealing. They could be both old and young. Harley and TJ watched their transformation in amazement.

At last, they faced their mother. "You need to judge the plea. We agree to the exchange."

Chapter 26

The Verdict

Though the Sisters of Fate agreed to the compact of life trades, Themis ordained one final addition to this compact. She had come to admire the tenacity of these young mortals. If they were reflective of the human race, maybe there was a chance for Muse Clio to preserve the relationship between the immortals and the mortals.

"You, Harley Delosian, son of Charlie and Valoria Delosian, and you, TJ Harris, son of Jason and Lydia Harris, have demonstrated honor, bravery, and loyalty beyond any mortal being before you. Therefore, during the life span you have been given, each time we perceive such attributes performed with sincerity, they will add thread to your tapestry until such time your mortal bodies can no longer function."

Hephaestus jumped up. "Samuel, only child of Niobe Crabtree, should be gifted the same opportunity, since now they are all brothers of a common thread."

The divine audience cheered in agreement.

"So be it," Themis judged. "These three mortals will be under observation henceforth. You are all responsible to report their achievements to this council for determination of the value of their acts."

Excited applause greeted her words; the boys hugged Hephaestus tightly.

"Thank you," they cried. "Thanks for remembering to include Sammy."

"I foresee that Sammy may outlive you all," he laughed.

"And that's perfectly okay with us," TJ said.

"Perfectly," Harley repeated. "Now let's find the cure." He reached into the pouch and grabbed the bloody ball of thread. "This is for you," he said with great respect. "Thank you for helping us."

A cloudy mist swept into the room. It was no longer dark and thunderous. Instead, a beautiful iridescent neon green light began wrapping around the three sisters. Lachesis held the bloody ball of thread close to her chest. "Remember your promise," she said as she and her siblings faded into the light and were swept away.

"Green, of course, the symbol of rebirth," Hephaestus observed the exit of the Moirae. "Where will you go next?"

"We receive a message on this parchment," Harley said, holding up the rolled object. "It tells us stuff we have to figure out."

"Then we plan our next move," TJ added.

"I am not skilled in the healing arts," Hephaestus said, "but tell me more about your sleeping friend."

"You tell him about the accident," Harley suggested, "and I'll tell him about the hospital."

"Okay," TJ began soberly. He wanted Hephaestus to know that he was responsible for Sammy's accident, even though Harley and Coach Kreller would disagree adamantly. "We play soccer, a football game where players try to maneuver a ball across a goal line. Sammy was on defense with me, trying to keep the other team from scoring. The shot was high, and because we not allowed to use our hands, Sammy was planning to attack the ball with his head. Then, somehow, he fell down and hit his head really hard on the ground."

Hephaestus listened carefully. "Mother Earth tries to gently embrace all life that arises from her form, but those lives that fall from above, she cannot predict their arrival, so she cannot prepare them a soft landing. I am sure she feels great sorrow for Sammy."

"The thing is," Harley picked up the story, "Sammy woke up in the hospital. He seemed normal and happy. And then he fell into a deep sleep. He would say things that neither his mother nor the doctors could make any sense of.

"If he awoke once," Hephaestus said, "and talked with you and then fell back into an even deeper slumber, then something else is going on. In this world there are dark spirits who act selfishly and often dangerously toward others, especially mortals who are essentially defenseless."

"That doesn't sound good," shuddered Harley, "but we can't let that get in our way. We have to try everything to complete our quest."

"Because you chose me as your counsel," Hephaestus explained, "Zeus has permitted me to grant you one wish or favor during your journey on this side." He looked sternly at both boys. "Think wisely before calling upon me—there is only one gift I can grant you."

"We understand," Harley responded, "but how do we call you?"

The god with massive muscles reached into the air and pulled into reality a pair of golden sandals. "When you wish to speak with me, I cannot come to you, so you must come to me. Put these sandals on your feet and you will be brought to me with the speed of the wind."

TJ held the sandals in front of him and studied their structure. "These look like any other sandals, except they are made of gold." As he said these words, the golden illumination faded away and the footwear looked like ordinary sandals.

"When one puts them on and ties the laces, the magical powers of the sandals will come alive again," explained the god. "The wearer cannot change his mind. Once the sandals are removed, the powers will dissolve."

Harley reached for the dull-colored sandals and stuffed them into the pouch. "We better get going, TJ."

"May all that is good and glorious from Mount Olympus be at your side and light your way," Hephaestus blessed them.

The boys nodded to him as his visage faded away. "We have another friend on this side," TJ said, recalling both Epimenides and the naiad. "Friends make difficult times more bearable."

The owl on Harley's amulet blinked. Apollo's crow cawed in the distance. The parchment in Harley's hand quivered slightly. He unrolled it and began to read aloud:

> "To the healer's daughter you must go
>
> Secure the ancient serpentine bowl
>
> With herbal nectar dripped from its lip
>
> A sleeping boy must soon take a sip."

Harley scratched his head and reread the message. "We already know this," he snapped. "Why doesn't it tell us something we don't know?"

"Maybe the person writing this doesn't know what we know."

"Okay, TJ," Harley conceded, "let's review what we know: We have to get Hygea's special bowl. Hygea is the daughter of Aesculapius, the great healer, and Aesculapius is the son of Apollo."

"That's it," TJ interrupted. "Apollo is the god of doctors. That's why the AMA uses a caduceus as their symbol."

"A what?"

"A staff with a snake wrapped around it," TJ explained. "Sometimes they show it with wings, because it first belonged to Hermes, the messenger of Zeus.

"Snakes again," hissed Harley. "Those ancient people sure had a fixation about snakes." He stepped carefully, hoping not to encounter one of those legless serpents, precious or otherwise.

They neared the foot of the giant mountain. The sun shone high above, but the air temperature was mild and comfortable. Keeping a safe distance between them, Korvus continued traveling with the friends. As if on cue, Korvus cawed to them. At the same instant,

Harley's owl amulet blinked. The boys stopped and Harley pulled the parchment from his pouch.

"What does it say?" asked TJ.

> "To her father's temple there remain
> Place your offering of silent grain
> Reaped with joy from venerated fields
> Life from her healing art you will yield."

Harley finished reading…

CHAPTER 27

The Harvest

Dr. Ammon reviewed Sammy's chart for a third time. "I don't understand it, Mrs. Crabtree," he finally said with hopeful exasperation. "Sammy's vital signs have stabilized. Though we can't wake him up, he seems to have reached stasis."

Mrs. Crabtree grabbed Nurse Fisher's hand. "Is he going to be okay?"

The nurse patted her hand warmly. "His condition has not deteriorated since last night."

"It's almost as if he has been given more time," Niobe Crabtree cried. "His body can use this time to get stronger." Her quivering voice was edged with a mother's hope. Samuel, the light of her life, was her only child; she loved him from the depth of her being and would readily give her life in exchange for his.

"We must move forward with caution," Dr. Ammon reminded them. "He's not out of the woods yet."

"But he's closer to the edge of those woods than he has been for days," Mrs. Crabtree responded. "My son is going to get well." She paused to explore his face with tearful eyes. "I can feel it in here." Niobe pounded her chest with her clenched fist.

As Dr. Ammon and Nurse Fisher left the room, they listened to Mrs. Crabtree singing a lullaby to her sweet boy. "If love alone could heal," the nurse whispered, "that boy would be up and running around with his friends."

"I'll tell you, Ursula, never underestimate the power of love in the field of healing."

"Okay, Harley, we have to know the name of the place we must go," TJ said.

"I think I remember this myth," Harley said, "because I thought it was sad that Demeter had only one or two stories about her life as an immortal. The most obvious one was when Hades ran off with her daughter Persephone, causing Demeter to mourn her loss so much that the world almost came to an end. I also remember that there was a mystery surrounding the five-year harvest of her corn. Ms. Clio called it the Eleusinian Mysteries because the temple celebration was done in total silence and no one who participated spoke about what went on.

"So that's the one," TJ jumped in. "The 'silent grain' is that corn. We have to get it and offer it to Aesculapius in his temple."

"Okay, so where are we going?"

"Demeter and Dionysus are the earth gods; her temple was outside of Athens in a small settlement called Eleusis."

So, once again, they sat in a circle joined by the leather thongs of their amulets. They both concentrated on a field of cornstalks. The air within the circle began to vibrate, gently at first. When it reached a fever pitch, they felt the change in air around them. At first they heard the rustle of leaves being tickled by playful breezes. Then they heard voices.

"Look, Harley," TJ said.

Harley opened his eyes to discover a crowd of laborers, each with a heavy sack hanging from a headband. These sacks were filled with cornhusks. They leaned forward as they walked, as if all were members of a puppetry parade. These were happy laborers, for they sang in unison a melody Harley could not decipher. It was almost like chanting.

"I think they're going to the festival," TJ whispered.

"Let's follow them."

Before long they found themselves among a larger gathering. The workers sat in different groups, performing different tasks of the harvest. Harley and TJ joined a circle of mostly women and girls, and waited. Two older girls about their age tittered at the sight of two boys joining the winnowing circle. They handed each boy a winnowing fan. They had no idea what to do with the woven implement.

In short order, another worker dumped a basket of kernels in the center of their circle. Each person with a winnowing fan began lifting the kernels into the air in rhythmic waves. Their fans created a breeze that lifted the chaff higher, blowing it away. All that remained were clean kernels of the precious corn.

TJ was the first to try his fan. He threw the kernels so high that they landed randomly all over the women next to him. The two girls covered their mouths with their hands trying to hold back their laughter.

It was Harley's turn. He tossed his pile more gracefully. Yet his winnowing motion still sent the kernels flying in every direction. This time the girls burst out laughing. Harley blushed two shades of red.

"Let us show you," one of the girls offered. Harley and TJ made room between them. She sat with legs crossed comfortably in lotus style, long skirt covering her knees modestly, as did all the other women.

She scooped a fanful of kernels and waved her winnowing fan firmly. The grain lifted no more than eight to ten inches above her fan. In a dance-like move, she caught the kernels as they were pulled back to the fan and flipped her wrist. As the flow fell back, the lightweight chaff was caught in the breeze. It blew higher into the air and was whisked away over the heads in the circle. They all moved in perfect rhythm, humming throughout the ritual. Their sound and their movements became mesmerizing. Harley and TJ swayed forward and back…forward and back.

Suddenly, it stopped. No song, no movement. They had finished their work. A different group stepped into the circle to gather the plaited mats now layered in colorful corn kernels. Before they retreated, they covered the ground with a clean spread of mats. The process of winnowing the grain began again.

"Harley, let's follow them," TJ suggested. "They might lead us to the temple."

The closer the group came to an outcropping of buildings, the quieter they became. Even the goats in flimsy corrals moved about in silence. The largest building reminded Harley of a barn without the loft. The lead worker stopped at the double doors. Harley thought the Olympians had palatial temples. If this was Demeter's temple, it was simple and rustic compared to the Parthenon of Athena.

The crowd stood in a semi-circle before the double doors. The leader raised a tray of corn to the sky. Then he turned in each direction, repeating the ritual as if invoking favor from the gods. In fact, he was honoring the rain, the wind, the sun, and the earth, thanking them for this harvest. As soon as he completed his circle offering of thanksgiving, the doors slowly opened.

A beam of intensely bright light shot out into the clearing. The boys jumped back, not sure what to do next. The crowd of worshippers sank to their knees in supplication. A mature, confident woman dressed in traditional royal attire stepped out of the light. Her hair was the color of cornsilk and her skin was a rich, sun-kissed bronze. Everywhere she stepped, tiny blossoms of purple flowers sprouted.

She walked, no, she floated among the worshippers. It was the Goddess of the Corn, the daughter of Kronos and Rhea, the sister of Zeus himself...she was Demeter. Graciously she reached out to touch the tops of bowed heads. Each supplicant she caressed seemed to glow like an LED bulb warming up.

She laid her warm gentle hand on Harley's head. A tingle shot through his body. "Harley Delosian, son of Charlie and Valoria Delosian, master of the canine Apollo, and friend of Samuel Crabtree, welcome." Then she turned to TJ. "Thomas Jarrell Harris, son of Jason and Lydia Harris, friend of Samuel Crabtree, I have been expecting you."

The boys looked quizzically at each other. Korvus flapped his ebony wings and gracefully landed on Demeter's shoulder. She offered it a kernel of her holy corn. While it crunched on its favorite treat, the goddess gently stroked its feathers.

"I thought farmers didn't like crows," Harley said in surprise.

"I think this one is special," TJ said. "It belongs to Apollo, after all."

"Come with me," ordered Demeter. She led the boys into the temple. The door closed behind them. It was definitely the home of the harvest. Every food plant the boys had ever imagined lined the crates along the walls. Potted flowers and twisting vines decorated the entire space. In the middle was a circular clearing. The floor had been brushed clean; no footprints could be seen.

"Is this your temple?" TJ asked?

Demeter placed her finger over her lips, indicating that no one speak. The flowers quivered at the essence of her being. They made their way around

the perimeter of the circle altar. She indicated an anteroom off to the side.

They followed her through the archway and found themselves in an expansive valley of flora. The grasses were greener, the trees were taller and fuller, the flowers showed every color of the rainbow, and the sky was blue…a beautiful, clear, vibrant blue.

"This is like a dream world," Harley said.

"It is my dream world," Demeter laughed. "Tell me about your people. I have not had the opportunity to visit your world, but my niece Clio told me much about it."

"Where do you want us to start?" asked TJ.

"Please," Harley begged. "I don't mean any disrespect, but we have to complete our quest if we are going to help our friend."

"I am aware of Samuel Crabtree's condition," Demeter said gently, "but the Moirae have kept their promise…his tapestry has been expanded with the ball of thread you gave to them." She turned to TJ. "So, indulge me for a few moments."

CHAPTER 28

TOUCH OF EARTH

"I AM PROFOUNDLY INTRIGUED," DEMETER announced. "You go to school for 12 years before you make life decisions, and in addition, both boys and girls are educated in the same classroom."

"Well, there are boys' schools and girls' schools, but we go to public school," TJ explained.

"And you don't study military techniques and strategies?"

The boys laughed. "The closest thing we have to that is P. E., or physical education, where we exercise and learn how to do physically competitive games like soccer, football, and basketball," Harley added.

"And the girls do these games in P. E. as well?"

"Sure, some girls are better than we are in some activities," TJ admitted. "You realize how envied you would be in this world," Demeter said. "Only boys from important families can go to school. Girls are usually taught household skills by their mothers, and boys are trained in military leadership, music, and philosophy."

"But some girls are really smart, like our friends Azlynn and Tamiko," TJ told her proudly. "Azlynn is a reader. I think she has read almost every book in our library."

Demeter threw her hands into the air and began spinning around. "You have a library? Can anyone have access to books in your library?"

Harley and TJ exchanged glances, wondering why something as mundane as a library excited this goddess. "We have a school library and a public library downtown. All anyone needs is a library card, and he or she can check out books to take home or read there in the library," Harley said.

"Then all your people must be extraordinarily well-informed and intellectually gifted."

"Why do you think that?" TJ wanted to know.

"You have masses of information right at your fingertips. I imagine that there are long lines of people waiting to check out books."

"Not actually," TJ stuttered shamefully. "Not many kids read books—only the ones assigned by teachers."

"And not even those, sometimes," Harley added.

"Are you saying that mankind has squandered its gifts and deteriorated into an empty shell of ignorance and apathy?" Demeter sank to her knees and began to sob. Every tear that fell to the earth produced a lovely flower.

After a few moments, the boys sat next to her, trying not to crush the new flowerbed. "I'm really sorry," Harley tried to assuage her agony, "that we created that impression in your mind."

"Actually," TJ redirected the conversation, "there are some modern people who are doing some amazing things, like planning flights to distant planets, curing diseases like AIDS and cancer, and so many other wonderful things that require bright minds and determination…these people had to have read books."

Demeter looked up, "You have so much and our mortal children have so little. I guess it's human nature to covet those things that others have that would make one's life better. Please take this wisdom and share it with other mortals: Recognize the gifts the Universe has put on your plate and feast on those that will cause you to grow and flourish, making your life and the lives of those around you more bountiful and more beautiful."

She reached into the sky and pulled something solid out of thin air. "In exchange for your gift of insight into the world so far away in time, I give you the gift of the Eleusinian Mysteries produced with a vow of silence."

Harley opened his pouch and watched as the Goddess of the Harvest placed a glowing ear of corn inside. She reached upward again. A magical hand opened before their eyes and a bunch of luscious grapes was passed from the hand of Dionysus to Demeter to the pouch. This was more than what they had expected.

Harley closed the pouch. "Goddess, we don't know how to thank you and Dionysus for your gifts."

"Your kindness may turn out to be the very thing that saves our friend back home," TJ said.

"Ms. Clio, your teacher, and Dionysus are family and my closest friends. I understand exactly how you feel." She placed a gentle hand on each of their heads. They bowed respectfully, closed their eyes, and prepared to feel the true warmth and joy of her touch, the touch of the earth.

"Remember what you have learned," she said softly. "Have a safe and fruitful journey."

The air around them glimmered like raindrops in the sunshine. They felt weightless and happy. It was true was Ms. Clio had told them about Demeter. She was a goddess who brought joy to the world and nourishment into the minds and hearts of mortals.

The sensation of moving, flying freely, abruptly stopped. Harley, still clutching the pouch, looked up. "TJ," he said, "open your eyes."

They were standing side by side next to a marble temple lined with makeshift cots. They were also standing in a pit of snakes.

"Don't move, Harley," TJ suggested. Even before TJ had spoken, Harley had had no intention of moving. For all he knew, he had even stopped breathing. A serpent sniffed his ankle with its tongue. Slowly it began to wind its way around his leg. Another curious snake showed interest in his other foot. The two snakes, no longer than twelve inches each, seemed to communicate with each other as they very slowly and smoothly wound their way upward.

Harley stood frozen. If, like dogs, snakes could smell fear, they would know that he was out of his mind with paralyzing terror. Without moving a muscle, Harley watched the snakes eye his face. They were moving, as if dancing, ever upward. When they reached his waist, they wrapped around Harley, head to tail. They circled him several times before resuming their ascent.

Harley's heart was pounding like a jackhammer. His breath was coming in short, desperate bursts. Somewhere in the back of his mind he heard… "No one knows the depths of his heroism until he faces his greatest fear." Harley was facing one of *his* greatest fears at this very moment.

The serpents around TJ crawled in and around and over and under again. None attempted to climb up his legs. Each time TJ tried to reach across to Harley, his nest of snakes became agitated and hissed angrily. TJ could see that his friend was in great distress.

"That's it," he said out loud to the writhing snakes. He reached across and gently lifted each unwanted explorer from Harley's body. TJ placed his thumb and forefinger behind their heads and pulled. At first the vipers did not want to release their grip. It was as if they were enjoying the tension they had created in their human climbing pole.

At last the nests of snakes seemed to lose interest, and began slithering off toward a structure which housed a group of people. A young woman in a long Grecian gown walked among them. She looked up and smiled at the boys and waved them forward. They stepped gingerly around the trail of snakes. When they were finally face to face with the young woman, they realized just how welcoming her countenance was.

"Hello," she greeted them, "I've been expecting you."

Chapter 29

Hygea

The people lying or sitting on the cots were sick. Some were wrapped in blood-soaked bandages. Others were covered in crusted skin sores or suffered a yellow viscous seepage from their eyes. There were as many men as there were women. Even a few children lay in some sort of agonizing malady.

The young woman seemed oblivious to the possibility of catching their viruses. She washed her hands in a bowl of clean water after treating each patient. With every sick person, she leaned in close and spoke in comforting tones. They were visibly uplifted by her caring, sincere approach. After her words, the patient would lie down quietly, as if in a trance. That's when Harley witnessed something that made his skin crawl.

The snakes slithered onto the cots of the sick and injured. Just as they had done with Harley, they wrapped themselves around the arms and legs and necks of each patient. Their serpent tongues flickered in and out. Whatever they drew from the air seemed to direct their movements.

An old man with oozing eyes didn't move as two determined snakes slid over his chin and cheekbones. Their tongues quivered as they approached his eyes. Harley wanted someone to run over to him and yank those snakes from his face. "They can kill him with their venom," Harley screamed inside his head.

"No, Harley Delosian." Having heard his thoughts, the young woman said to him, "They are curing him."

Harley turned to the woman in surprise. "I didn't say anything."

"Harley, your thoughts speak quite loudly."

"So, the snakes are like medicine?" asked TJ.

"Even in your world, venom is used as a medicinal cure…snake venom…bee venom…venom from creatures of the sea," the woman explained. My name is Hygea, child of Aesculapius the great healer and son of almighty Phoebus Apollo."

"It is an honor to meet you at last," TJ said. "We have been on a quest and you are the end of our journey."

"I know who you are," she comforted TJ, who was almost brought to tears, "and I know what you seek."

"Can you help us…can you help Sammy?" Harley begged. "I'm worried that we are running out of time."

"We have to get back to Sammy with medicine that will wake him up," added TJ.

"Do you do this alone?" asked Hygea.

"Alone?" Harley repeated. "Sammy has many friends who love him. His mother is devoted to him." He looked to TJ, "We are here, but we are not alone in our quest."

"We have two very close friends and Harley's dog waiting for us back home," TJ explained.

"Azlynn and Tamiko," said Hygea.

"How…how did you know?" stammered Harley.

"They are good friends," Hygea stated. "You are quite fortunate and I anticipate that you will remain close friends for years to come."

She turned toward a modest structure on the hillside. "Follow me," she ordered.

The people, the cots, and most importantly, the snakes seemed to have been absorbed into a bright light. Harley and TJ followed Hygea up the hill. Their anticipation was at its peak. Hygea was the promise of the cure for Sammy Crabtree's deep sleep.

"You realize what has happened…do you not?"

"Happened to us or to Sammy?" Harley asked.

"To Samuel Crabtree, of course; he is the target of our attention."

"All we know is that for some reason, that not even the doctors can figure out, he can't wake up. So he is getting weaker and his body is shutting down," offered TJ.

"It all began with a head injury during a soccer game," said Harley.

"There is so much more to his malady than you have imagined," Hygea said firmly. "The offspring of Morpheus have selected Samuel Crabtree to join their slumber life and to entertain the elder deity."

"Our teacher, Ms. Clio, told us about the gate of dreams," TJ said. "The one made of horn gives true dreams, but the other one, the ivory one, sends false dreams."

"Death, the brother of Sleep, lives beyond the Acheron, the river of woe, and the Cocytus, the river of lamentation," explained Hygea. "He constantly reaches for the sick and the lonely…while I and my siblings strive to heal those who could fall easy prey to Death and his companions."

"That sounds awful," Harley realized out loud. "Hygea, we have to keep Sammy from becoming a victim."

TJ was even more anxious. "Sammy can't die…he just can't."

"Morpheus is the god of slumber and the son of Hypnos, the god of sleep. He is a shape-shifter and often takes on forms to deceive his victims before he puts them into an eternal slumber."

"Did he cause this to happen to Sammy?" Harley asked.

"I am not of such status to know for sure," Hygea answered, "but it sound like and feels like his work."

"Can you make something to cure Sammy?" TJ cried.

"Use your magic bowl, the one with snakes around the bowl, to mix up some kind of medicine," Harley pleaded.

The boys had believed that their entire quest was a guarantee that this person from a world so far away in time and place had the answers to their search. Now, doubt was beginning to worm its way into their once-firm, protective shell of hope.

"I have this for you," Harley said, handing the pouch to Hygea. "Maybe it can help."

With the precision of a surgeon, Hygea opened the pouch and examined its contents. "Let's go inside my home," she invited, "and we will begin."

The inside of her home was much more spacious than its outside suggested. A pile of coals glowed in the hearth, heating a cauldron of bubbly liquid. The essence of lavender filled their nostrils. Though it was dark inside, it was pleasant and felt safe. The walls were lined with a myriad of containers and tied bunches of various dried plants. Hygea's worktable was neat and orderly.

She reached beneath the table and hoisted a dusty tome onto the tabletop. With dexterity, she flipped through the pages until she found what she was looking for. Hygea read through the ancient text line by line. "This recipe, handed down by ancient deities, offers variations. I must be precise in my measurements and with my ingredients."

Harley and TJ watched with fascination. Hygea moved to a shelf and carefully selected an array of wooden spoons and bowls. She aligned them according to size on her table. Once again, she ran her finger over the writing. She walked along the wall of containers, pulling out this one and that one filled with unknown tinctures and concoctions of powders that the boys couldn't imagine.

Finally, she reopened Harley's pouch. She reached inside and pulled out a small bunch of juicy grapes. "This will make a difference in our potion."

"Is that a good thing?" TJ asked.

"Or does that complicate things?" Harley questioned her.

"Apothecary art requires an understanding of how things in nature combine and what that combination means for healing."

"And the grapes?" Harley blurted louder than he intended.

"The drops of grape nectar, especially these grapes offered from the hand of the god of the vine, increase the positive effects of the potion—by enhancing the energy of the tiny white sprites that dance throughout the mortal body."

"That's a good thing," TJ decided.

"Yes, it is…if combined with one more element that I do not have here."

Hygea gently squeezed the juice from several grapes. Then she pulled several kernels from the ear of corn that continued to glow in the dimly lit room. She lovingly pinched each kernel, forcing a milky liquid to flow over her fingers into a bowl.

Hygea began to chant, using words and phrases unknown to the boys. They recognized the sounds of a repeated phrase. Each time she spoke those words, she added precise amounts of a different element, be it liquid or powder, to the bowl of grape juice and corn milk. Finally, Hygea stopped chanting. She uncovered a beautifully carved bronze chalice and placed it like a centerpiece.

"That's it," Harley exclaimed. "That's the one we learned about…Hygea's cup!"

"Before I pour this potion into the healing cup, I need one more element that only you can secure." She handed the precious cup to Harley. "The healing snakes must bless this bowl with their essential oils."

Harley was stupefied. The more forcefully Hygea pushed the bowl in his direction, the more insistent he was at pushing it back. He wanted nothing more to do with those snakes.

"Harley," she began, "you descend from a proud race of mortals who protected and sheltered Leto so that Apollo and Artemis could come to full term and be born. Your ancestors were brave. They lived on an island that floated. From one day to the next, they did not know if they would survive the perils of Poseidon or of Aeolus, King of the Winds. Yet, they not only endured—they thrived even though the island seemed rocky and barren. The moment Leto stepped foot on this floating island, four huge pillars rose from deep beneath the sea and anchored the island, birthplace of Apollo and Artemis."

She stared directly into Harley's eyes. "It is their blood that runs through your body. It is their courage to do the right thing that fills your soul." She pushed the bowl harder into his hands. "Be who you were destined to be."

Reluctantly, Harley wrapped his fingers around the stem upon which the bowl was set. "I can do this," he said, trying to convince the scared little boy who lived in his subconscious. He walked out the door of the hut into the welcoming light of day.

"I'll help," offered TJ.

Hygea held him back. "He must do this on his own. While we wait, tell me more about your friends who await your return."

TJ looked toward Harley who was walking at a slow but steady pace and then back at Hygea. "He'll be okay—won't he?"

CHAPTER 30

Waiting

WAITING IS THE WORST thing ever, but if you are a dog, a faithful companion such as Apollo, it is what you do most of the time, anyway.

"Should we begin to worry?" Tamiko asked.

"Begin?" Azlynn laughed. "I was worried the moment we agreed to do this with them."

"You know we would've joined them no matter what."

"You're right," Azlynn agreed. "It's a pretty good feeling to know that you have friends—really close friends like we all are." Apollo looked up and wagged his tail furiously. "Yes, and you, too, Apollo," Azlynn continued. "You are probably the best friend of all."

"Do you realize that he hasn't left that spot since they disappeared into the portal?"

"Do you think he understands what's going on?" Azlynn asked, scratching behind Apollo's ears.

"Woof."

"He understands enough," Tamiko said. "He's a really smart dog."

"Woof! Woof!"

"I think he agrees," Azlynn laughed.

"Azlynn," Tamiko said, "I was wondering. If you could sit down and talk to anyone from history, who would you pick and why?"

"Anyone?" she repeated. "Actually, I've thought about this and there are several people who fascinate me." A thoughtful forefinger tapped an unidentifiable rhythm on her cheek. "I know I'd like to spend a couple hours with Emily Dickinson."

"Why her?"

"She seemed to be a really private person, but she liked people who came to her house. I understand her poetry. You know she didn't live long enough to realize just how famous her words would become. I think that's kind of sad. I want to tell her about her poetry that we read in school. I think she would be pleased—in a humble sort of way."

Both girls contemplated the image of Azlynn and Emily Dickinson having tea in Victorian china cups, talking about poetry in the Dickinson parlor.

"What about you, Tamiko," Azlynn challenged, "what living person would you want to spend time with?"

"A living person," mused Tamiko. "I know I'm going to sound like a groupie or something…but…I'd like to visit with Michelle Obama, because she is just one of the smartest, most articulate women alive. And she seems genuine. You know what I mean?"

"I've watched political speeches and live interviews with her and I agree. She's got it together," Azlynn nodded.

"I want to hear from her what it was like when she was our age. I want to know how she dealt with bullies and disappointment," Tamiko said, imagining an infinite list of conversational topics. "Most of all, I want to know if her life turned out the way she planned."

"Do you think Mrs. Obama would actually sit down and talk to middle school kids like us?" Azlynn wondered.

"I think she would," Tamiko decided, "and I think she would be very honest with us."

"Do you think Michelle would like to talk with Emily?"

"Now, you're stretching it," laughed Tamiko. "But I think the former First Lady would enjoy tea, and I think Emily would enjoy hearing about public life in Washington, D. C. for an African-American, educated woman."

The air above the circle seemed to be getting thicker. "Something's happening," Tamiko realized.

They straddled the circle to watch and wait. The atmosphere had changed. Maybe the boys were on their way back.

Harley continued walking. He would face his fear alone. The snakes were back; dozens of them writhed in sheer joy with their brethren. Harley told himself, "Breathe, suck in the air through your mouth—exhale through your nose." To protect his sanity, Harley disengaged from the actual event as a participant, instead being an observer. He intended to talk to himself, guiding himself through the terror.

"You're doing great, Harley," he said. "You haven't passed out—yet."

The snakes stopped moving. Harley's foot stood firmly in their midst. Then he planted his other foot in their nest without harming a single snake. They all eyed each other like two gangs of gunfighters at the OK Corral. Who would be the first to strike?

"Harley," his voice snapped him back to his mission, "they can't coat the bowl unless you give it to them."

Harley abruptly but carefully lowered his body into a seated position among the snakes. They began to quiver as if asking each other what this crazy kid was up to. Harley locked his ankles and lowered the precious cup between his legs. He was determined not to release it.

The bowl created excitement in the nest. The snakes began moving in every direction to reach it. Harley felt them crawling over his bare legs, crawling up his back and over his shoulders. His survival urge was to scream and run away, but something inside his head had taken control. He could regulate his breathing so as not to alarm the snakes. He even closed his eyes.

A curious snake crawled up his arm and rested against his ear. Then it began to explore Harley's face. Like a diadem, it wrapped around the crown of his head. Still, he did not move. The snake was testing him. While the others crawled in and out of the bronze bowl, this snake remained focused on his head.

Harley felt the constant darting of the snake's tongue. "You are brave," an imaginary voice whispered into his ear. "We know you detest our kind and that sitting among us is the most frightening thing you've ever done."

His lips didn't move, but Harley was thinking out loud. "You are the instrument of healing and I need your help. How can I fear what I need the most?"

"Do you not fear losing your friend to death?" the snake whispered. "After all, you know death…do you not?"

"I know that my friend will have a better chance if we complete our quest. I have learned to set my fears aside for him."

"Friendship like that is rare, Harley Delosian," the snake hissed. "My brothers have coated Hygea's Bowl with medicinal magic. You can go now. Do not tarry. The grains of sand that count the minutes of your friend's day continue to fill the bottom of the hourglass."

Harley opened his eyes. He realized that the only snake that remained active was the one around his neck. "Take with you this message: All life serves a purpose on this earth. It is the duty of mankind to serve, protect, and cherish that life. You show them the way, Harley Delosian, son of Charlie and Valoria Delosian."

A short distance away, Hygea continued probing TJ for information. "I think I like this Tamiko person," Hygea told TJ. "She has the mind of a healer and the heart as well."

"Tamiko is always so worried about missing a step in her carefully planned life that she doesn't have fun like other kids."

"It is you, her friend, who will build her confidence," Hygea explained. "Stand tall next to her. Be there should she trip and be there when she dares to relax. No one will ever understand her the way you do, the way all her special friends do."

Harley stepped through the door of the hut. TJ and Hygea stared at him, waiting for him to speak. He extended the hand that held the cup. "It has been properly blessed," he said.

"Are you okay, Harley?" TJ worried.

"I am fine, but I am not the same person who walked out the door a few minutes ago."

"I see that," TJ said. "You seem different…again."

Chapter 31

The Gift

TJ KNEW THAT PEOPLE could be changed dramatically when faced with a traumatic or emotionally charged experience. He had read about and watched stories on the History Channel about historic people who claimed to have undergone such a change. It was possible that Harley had been through two such events that somehow impacted his basic nature—first inside the Labyrinth, and now with the snakes. The Harley he knew back home was carefree and fun-loving most of the time. This Harley had become deeper and more serious. There was a look in his eyes that told TJ he was not the same kid who began this quest with him. TJ began to question whether he, too, had changed.

Hygea finished her work. Reverently, she poured the mixture into her bowl. "Now, you can offer this potion to Samuel Crabtree and he will awaken." The boys grinned from ear to ear. They had done it. Sammy would be okay. "However," she continued, "if you wish to offer your friend more than wakefulness, there is one more element to be added."

"We can do more for Sammy?" Harley questioned.

"One more element?" TJ repeated.

"You can offer Samuel robust health that he can sustain throughout his life."

"Are you telling us that if we add that missing element, Sammy might never be sick again?" Harley asked with growing optimism.

"Your friend will be blessed with more than a strong body," Hygea said. "He will be able to accomplish more than he believes. His spirit will soar and all around him will bask in his energy and joy."

"Harley," TJ addressed his friend, "there's no option here. If Sammy can be gifted such a life, then we have to get this last element for his potion."

"What is the thing we have to find?" Harley turned to Hygea.

"You must fill the bowl with exactly 14 tears of Niobe. Once that is done, this healing potion can be drunk by your friend."

"Tears of Niobe?" both boys repeated in unison.

Hygea retells the story of Niobe and Tantalus:

No mortal or half-mortal had ever been invited to dine with the gods until Tantalus, the celebrated son on Zeus, was allowed to enjoy their ambrosia and drink their nectar. They loved him so much that they even agreed to dine with him in his palace.

For reasons unknown, Tantalus had become possessed. He wanted to show that even the gods could be deceived, so he decided to serve a bizarre and horrific feast with his own son, Pelops, as the main course. All but one of the immortal guests, Demeter, knew what Tantalus had done, but she unknowingly consumed a part of the shoulder of the murdered son.

In consequence, Tantalus was banished to the Underworld of Hades. Here he was placed in a pool of water that would shrink away every time he tried to quench the thirst that tormented him. Fruit trees grew near enough for Tantalus to abate his hunger, offering figs, sweet pears, luscious pomegranates, and shiny apples. Each time he reached for nourishment, winds would cast the fruit just out of his reach. His eternal punishment was to be within reach of his desires, but never able to secure that which would quench his thirst or satisfy his hunger.

The gods took pity on Pelops and restored his body. They had Hephaestus construct a shoulder of ivory to replace the missing piece. Pelops lived a successful, happy life, even winning the hand of Princess Hippodamia.

Her father, having superior horses from Ares, challenged her suitors to a chariot race. Losing the race meant death to the suitor. Pelops was determined to win, and unbeknownst to the king, Pelops had been gifted horses from Poseidon himself. He won the race and the hand of Hippodamia.

Later, Pelops found out that the princess had caused a stable hand to sabotage the chariot wheels of the king, causing him to be dragged to his death. Pelops cursed and fatally punished the stable hand, thus continuing the misfortunes of the house of Tantalus.

Niobe was the daughter of Tantalus. She married Amphion, son of Zeus and a great musician. With his twin brother, Zethus, they moved the huge rocks to build the walls of Thebes with the music of Amphion's lyre. Amphion and Niobe became rulers of Thebes, living in great prosperity. Niobe relished her noble birth, great wealth, and her fertility, having borne seven sons and seven daughters—the fairest children ever born. But in her hubris, she suggested her subjects should worship her, not Leto, mother to Apollo and Artemis, mocking her for only having two children, while she had fourteen. Her insolence reached the ears of Leto's twins.

Together, Apollo and Artemis sent their arrows into the hearts of all of Niobe's children in retribution. She watched each of her children die. The impact of her loss, punished by the gods for her own arrogance, was beyond anything she could live with. Niobe fell to her knees and cried. Frozen, only her tears moved, flowing copiously. She was turned to stone and borne on a whirlwind to her native mountain where her tears continue to flow.

"The tears of Niobe," Harley said. "We can do this."

"Goddess," asked TJ, "do we have enough time?"

"All I can tell you is that you must hurry," said Hygea. "Fourteen drops …no more…no less."

Harley watched as Hygea placed the bowl inside his pouch. "Won't it spill?"

"Not yet. When you add the tears of Niobe," she explained, "it might become a problem."

"Why?" TJ asked.

"These are the tears of an unworthy woman," Hygea said without compassion. "Though her loss was great, her motives were selfish and presumptuous. Her tears are not protected by the Olympians."

"Why do her tears change your potion?" TJ continued his questions.

"They are genuine tears of a mother's pain," she said. "A mother's tears are powerful."

Harley remembered how long his own mother had cried when his father died. She had told him that she cried not only for the loss of her husband, but also cried for him, her son, who would never know his father beyond this moment in his life. Harley had had one of life's epiphanies: *Her tears were powerful, making him realize that he had to do more; he had to grow up.*

"Goddess," Harley spoke, "where will we find this crying stone called Niobe?"

"In the region of western Phrygia, her girlhood home, you will find a blue-green rock on Mount Sipylus, from which a stream flows. The people in the village drink not from this water, for they are shamed to be the final resting place for such a queen as Niobe. You must say nothing to them about your purpose. They must not know you have taken the tears. In their eyes, the shame of Niobe must not be allowed to spread beyond their borders."

Harley heard Korvus calling to him. "TJ, we've got to go…now."

"Thank you, goddess, for everything you have done for us and for everything you have taught us," TJ said with sincerity.

Chapter 32

Tears

Harley and TJ found a grassy area away from Hygea's hut. They sat in their circle position and readied their minds for another transport.

"Harley," TJ said, "this might be our last stop. We will soon be on our way home."

"I know. And if we can pull this off, we will have made a difference in Sammy's life."

"This is a big deal, Harley."

"Boy, you can say that again."

They closed the circle, then closed their eyes. They envisioned a natural rock formed on a mountain in the ancient region of Phrygia. The feeling of weightlessness was familiar and welcome. They were on the last leg of their quest before going home. Neither of them knew how much time had passed. In this world, the sky was always blue and the sun always shone brightly.

When the air relaxed, they opened their eyes at the same time. Everywhere they looked were nothing but trees. Even though the sky directly above them was a deep, cerulean blue, the land around them was shrouded in shadow. Trees of every size stood like a stately phalanx of hoplites protecting a royal perimeter.

"Do we have to go through there?" TJ asked.

"I think so," Harley answered, looking around. "It seems we are right in the middle."

A huge black bird flew from one branch to another. Korvus had been with them every step of the way. Maybe, they had decided, it was Apollo's way of helping them without actually helping them himself. It made sense. At the Council of the Olympians, Apollo seemed to be on their side. Of course, they had no idea what went on before or even after their arrival.

"Well, I don't think we have any other choice," TJ said. "Let's follow the bird."

They walked for what seemed like hours, the whole time looking high into the trees to make sure Korvus was still in sight.

Detecting an unusual scent, TJ said, "I smell something… something different in the air."

Harley breathed deeply through his nose. "Yes, it smells like a campfire and something cooking."

In a clearing just ahead they spotted an opening in the trees. Civilization.

The earth had been trampled into a path going to and from the settlement. "Do you think this is the place?" TJ wondered aloud.

Harley shrugged, searching for the bird which was nowhere to be seen.

A child stepped into their path. He couldn't have been more than five or six years old. He held out his little hand until TJ took hold of it. The child turned toward the village compound, taking the two young strangers along.

The child was insistent that they follow him. Like all ancient settlements, a public hearth burned hotly in the center of the main section of town. Women were pulling out loaves of coarse bread; a familiar, comforting smell wafted towards them. TJ's mother often baked loaves of bread. She would invite his friends over for a slice of hot bread smothered in creamy butter and sweet, sticky honey.

As they followed their guide down the narrow pathways between buildings, Harley caught a glimpse of something quite blue or unusually green, rising above the trees. He noted the landmarks around the area so he and TJ could find it again. The child finally stopped at a rough-looking hut with a carefully cleared yard around it.

"Mamma," called the boy.

A woman came to the door. She studied Harley and TJ. Then, as is the custom in Greece, she invited them to sit for a feast. The boy sat with the guests and smiled broadly. "Perdix," he said proudly, indicating himself.

"TJ," said TJ, touching his chest, then pointed to his friend, "Harley."

The boy repeated their names and laughed every time. The sound vibrations of their names in his mouth seemed to tickle his tongue. The mother returned with a tray of fruits and nuts. It was quite elaborate. They didn't appear to be wealthy, yet this tray was rich enough for a king.

She indicated for them to eat using the universal gesture of fingers to mouth. Neither she nor the boy ate from the tray, they simply watched with great pleasure as TJ and Harley consumed the delights presented to them. The mother was a kind, respectful hostess, and TJ and Harley were appropriately thankful, gracious guests. The gods would be pleased.

With his belly full, Harley sat back and looked around. It was a simple settlement without garish adornments. All of the walkways were swept clean. Very few people were visible. Most were women and children. It was at this moment Harley realized that these people were wearing bluish-green gemstones in their hair, around their wrists and ankles, and hanging from thin bands around their necks.

"TJ," he nudged and whispered, "look at those stones in their jewelry." TJ examined the stones without appearing rude. "What do they remind you of?"

"It looks like the stones Southwestern Native Americans wear," he said. "It's turquoise."

"That's what I thought," Harley agreed. "Do you think that it's the stone that Hygea told us about?"

"Well, it is a blue-green color," TJ said, "but does it cry?"

"You know that I've been collecting rocks," Harley began. "I started in 4th grade for a science project. Well, I enjoyed studying my rocks so much that I have been collecting ever since then."

"Did you study turquoise?"

"I did, because it seemed so important to tribal people in western North America. I know it exists in China, and in ancient Greece. People in ancient Egypt wore it. The name, turquoise, is actually French for Turkish, because Turkey is the country who introduced turquoise to Europe."

"Whoa," said TJ excitedly, "and if I'm remembering the ancient world maps in Ms. Clio's room correctly, Phrygia, where we were supposed to go, is part of modern-day Turkey! So we must be in the right place, but if it's the stone we're looking for, what does crying have to do with it?"

"I remember reading that turquoise is the by-product of the dehydration of a combination of other chemicals, including copper and feldspar, and that it's porous, related to limestone."

"So, the stone has to 'cry out' the moisture inside to make turquoise."

Harley realized that TJ was exactly right. The crying stone of Niobe probably contained turquoise. Now they had to find the source of it here in this settlement. Harley knew where to begin his search. They needed exactly 14 teardrops, and no one could know that they had taken them. He felt a little guilty about planning to deceive such welcoming people. He shared his concern with TJ.

"Harley," TJ tried to console him, "don't you think they would give us the tears if we had the time to explain what it was for?"

"I don't know," Harley worried. "Hygea was quite emphatic about doing this with total secrecy."

Perdix realized that they were speaking about something quite serious to them. He was polite enough not to eavesdrop, but he wanted to be helpful. He got up and walked over to TJ and once again took his hand. "Come," he repeated, "come with Perdix," indicating he'd show them the village.

"TJ," Harley muttered, "point to the turquoise and try to get him to show us where it comes from."

TJ pointed to the green stone hanging around the woman's neck, and told her it was beautiful. He then turned to the boy and asked where they found something so beautiful. The child again smiled broadly and pulled at TJ, anxious to show him the way. They followed him back on the same path that had brought them to his hut. Halfway there, Perdix turned down another street and into a clearing at the foot of a mountain.

There it was…an outcropping of stone partway up the hill, around which a pool of clear water collected and flowed into a small stream. Sections of the stone were definitely blue-green, parts of which had been chipped away. Upon a closer look, Harley saw a tiny droplet take form at the edge of a tiny crevice. As he watched, the droplet fell slowly into the pool that quickly absorbed it into its watery embrace.

"Look, TJ," he said in amazement, "the stone cries."

CHAPTER 33

Close Call

Harley and TJ stared at the beautiful stone for several minutes. Perdix became anxious, not understanding their fascination with the blue rock. He pulled at TJ again, "Come."

Resisting his tugging, TJ indicated that he and Harley were tired. He placed his clasped hands next to his cheek and closed his eyes. Perdix, even though a small boy, understood their need for a nap. He said, "Sleep, yes," and lay on the earth immediately, ready to sleep. TJ looked to Harley, realizing that if he lay down next to the boy and pretended to sleep, Harley would be free to collect the tears.

Harley watched TJ and figured out his plan. Harley moved a little to the far side of the pool and found a spot to lie down. Perdix seemed satisfied that everyone was going to take an afternoon nap.

After several minutes, Harley peeked over to see TJ and Perdix with their eyes closed. Without making a sound, he pulled the bowl from his pouch. It was as Hygea had prepared it. He paused, waiting to see if Perdix opened his eyes. He didn't. Harley raised his body slowly so as not to disturb the air around them. As he stood fully upright, he saw something that had not been clearly visible from the angle of their original approach to the pool. From this perspective at the side of the rock, he could definitely see the profile of a woman—Niobe, weeping for the loss of her children?

He had to catch himself from gasping aloud and waking Perdix. He couldn't wait to tell TJ and Tamiko and Azlynn and Ms. Clio what he'd seen.

Harley shook his head, getting back to the task at hand. He scanned the area looking for any movement. They were alone. He raised the bowl right below the fissure from which the last teardrop had fallen. It felt like forever before the next drop appeared. He maneuvered the bowl so that it would capture the drop. Then he waited some more. *One*, he thought soundlessly.

At least 20 seconds passed before the next tear began to seep from the stone. *Two*. Several minutes later, Perdix was beginning to stir. TJ had actually fallen asleep. Harley couldn't figure out a way to alert him without awakening Perdix too soon. *Ten*.

The situation was becoming precarious. Perdix was stretching his legs. He would open his eyes any second. *Eleven*. In his mind, Harley was screaming at TJ to wake up. Harley tried to place his body so that if Perdix woke up, he wouldn't be able to see what Harley was doing. *Twelve*.

Harley was desperate. He stretched his foot and made contact with TJ. He lost his balance a little and had taken his eyes off the rock. TJ sat up. Perdix sat up. TJ stretched his arm so wide that Perdix could not clearly seen what Harley was doing next to the weeping rock. Another drop fell into the bowl. *Is that 13 or did I miss 13 and that was 14?* Harley didn't know the answer. He pulled the bowl away.

"TJ," Harley said nervously, "tell Perdix good-bye. Let's get going."

"Everything okay?" TJ asked, then turning to bid the boy farewell.

"Yeah, I think so." The guilt and anxiety over not knowing for sure what the final count was began to grow inside Harley's heart. *Was it 13 or 14?* "It is what it is," Harley said. "I hope we're good."

They walked quickly but carefully back into the trees. This time there was no black bird to guide them. They were moving on adrenaline and instinct. Finally, they stopped.

"Do you know where we are?" TJ asked.

"I have no idea," confessed Harley. "Let's take a break and plan our next move."

"Our next move is going home."

"I don't think it's going to be that easy."

TJ was disappointed. "Why not?"

"Ms. Clio said that nothing from our world could be brought into this world, except for these," he said, fingering his amulet. "So it stands to reason that nothing from this world can be taken into ours."

"Well, how do we get the potion to Sammy?"

Something rustled the bushed near them. "Just a forest creature," Harley assured his friend. "Like a rabbit or a squirrel."

"Or like a bear or a wolf?"

"Come on, TJ, let's not borrow trouble here."

Suddenly, Korvus cawed and the owl on Harley's amulet blinked, "I know—another message." He set the pouch on the ground gingerly. He reached in, careful not to spill the bowl, and retrieved the scroll. Sure enough, a new message was slowly revealing itself on the page:

> Beware the sons of Oceanus.
>
> Whose thievery has run among us.
>
> You must seal the bowl, lose not a drop.
>
> The sleep of a friend you now can stop.

"Who is it talking about?" asked Harley.

"Oceanus was one of the original beings, the Titans," explained TJ. "I don't know anything about him."

"Well, his sons are thieves that we have to watch out for."

"How are we going to seal the bowl?" TJ asked.

"There's sure no plastic wrap or wax or anything I know of that can seal the top of this bowl," Harley said in frustration. "I knew it was too good to be true that we were almost home."

Korvus continued to caw at them, but owl stayed motionless. The bushes on the other side of them rustled again. Their nerves were on edge.

"Maybe that bird is telling us that we are about to be attacked," TJ said, looking over his shoulder.

"Remember what Hephaestus said," Harley reminded him. "He said we have one call or one wish that he will grant if it is in his domain."

TJ got excited. "That's right. He's the engineer on Mount Olympus. He can make anything."

"How do we contact him? "Let's just holler his name," TJ said. Then he began shouting. "Hephaestus! God of the forge and fire, please come to us, we need your help!" He waited and watched. A smoky cloud with crimson sparks popping inside as it materialized floated down from the trees. The muscle-bound god with the hammer and anvil appeared before them."

"How can I help you, young mortal friends?"

Chapter 34

Brothers

TJ jumped and ran to the god. "Hephaestus, we are so glad to see you."

"Yes," Harley said. "We have secured the potion that will heal our friend, Sammy, but we have a problem."

"And you think I can help with this problem."

"You are the craftsman of Mount Olympus," TJ said respectfully. "Can you craft a seal over the bowl that holds the healing potion so that it won't spill before it gets to Sammy?"

Hephaestus waved his fingers indicating that they should give him the bowl. He held it close to his eyes to examine its measurements and design. Finally, he set it on the ground and smiled broadly at them.

"This is your request?" he asked. "You may ask for only one. Remember?"

Harley and TJ locked stares. Both came to the same conclusion. "Yes," they said in unison.

"I will take it with me while you find your way out," Hephaestus said.

"Worry not…I will know where you are." With that, he returned to the smoky cloud and vanished above the trees.

Harley and TJ were so caught up in the spectacle of the god's ascent that they didn't see or hear the two mischievous creatures slip out from the bushes and advance toward the spot where they stood.

A branch snapped. Harley turned around. "Oh, no!" he yelled. Two long-armed, long-legged, monkeylike creatures snatched the pouch and began running back through the bushes. They scampered across the ground like squirrels.

Harley ran after them. TJ followed. The monkey-men laughed maniacally, tossing the pouch back and forth.

"TJ!" Harley yelled, "we have to get it back!"

"But there's nothing in it," TJ panted.

Harley held the parchment in his hand and Hephaestus had the bowl, yet Harley had a feeling that the pouch, which was a gift from one of the gods and had magical powers, was important to the end of their quest. "TJ," he grunted, "we were told to watch out for them for a reason." He was assuming these were the sons of Oceanus.

The monkey-men shot up a tall tree and sat high above them, sneering at their stupidity. They opened the pouch and began to dig inside looking for treasures.

They were sorely disappointed. Just as TJ had noted, the pouch was empty, so they began to play with it. The spindly creatures reached in and out of the pouch, even propping it on their heads making it a hat.

All Harley and TJ could do was watch their antics. "I can't believe I let them steal it," Harley berated himself.

"You didn't let them, Harley," TJ said, "they are good at stealing things.

The message said that they stole from both gods and men. So don't feel so bad."

One monkey was hanging from his tail that was wrapped around a narrow branch. It was swinging the pouch like an upside-down umbrella. The other was jumping up and down and shrieking. It wanted its turn with the toy. Unexpectedly, it reached over and yanked the strap of the pouch, causing the first monkey-man to lose its balance and grip on the branch. It began to tumble through the other branches, screaming as it fell.

The second monkey, now in possession of the pouch, laughed mockingly as its brother plummeted wildly downward. On the highest branch of the tree, Korvus cawed and cawed, as if yelling at the boys to do something about the situation. CAW!

Harley ran to stand under the tree to catch the monkey if it fell all the way through. It didn't. It latched on to a particularly bare branch and stopped its descent. It was angry and immediately stretched its spidery arm upward and grasped a higher branch.

The monkey-brother climbed with haste and determination. The other brother was lying on its back spinning the pouch with its feet as if it were a beach ball. It was having such a good time that it didn't notice the other mischief-maker advancing quickly.

Slam! The climber launched itself with furious force and landed smack dab in its brother's midsection. Both creatures shrieked and pulled violently at each other's fur, tearing out tufts and throwing them into the wind. Their sibling combat was just the ticket. The pouch slipped from their grasp and fell perfectly into Harley's outstretched arms.

Harley waved the pouch to TJ, indicating that they should slip away quickly and quietly. The fighters in the tree began chasing each other. They were so involved with winning the battle that they didn't notice that the two humans were no longer there.

"That was close," TJ sighed. "Those two spider monkeys were sons of Oceanus? I don't get it." They walked on in silence, thinking about where they were and how they got here. They thought about why they were there. Most of all, they thought about going home.

Korvus cawed to them as he flew ahead. Then, Harley's owl blinked.

"Why would we get another message," he wondered. "Aren't we done as soon as Hephaestus returns?"

They stopped and checked the space around them. No monkey-men.

Harley unrolled the parchment. They both watched the ink appear as letters—then words:

Apollo's fellow once white now black.

Will purvey the gift inside its pack.

A boy will catch in elusive flight.

In dreams a bonded friendship makes right.

TJ was first to speak. "He's Apollo's fellow." Korvus cawed. "The myth says he was white until he made Apollo unhappy. That's when Apollo turned him black as a reminder of his anger."

"So, the bird's going to deliver the bowl with the potion to Sammy?" asked Harley. "That makes sense, because you and I can't take anything back."

"He's going to do it in Sammy's dream," smiled TJ. "That's cool."

"When I talked to Sammy that time he woke up, he told me about the crow and said we had to catch it." Harley was still worried about the number of teardrops inside the potion. "TJ," he said somberly, "I got something to tell you."

"What's that?"

"Well, remember back at the pool?"

"Yeah."

"Well..." He couldn't continue because Hephaestus was on his way back. The cloudy transport lowered him to the ground. Hephaestus proudly stretched out his hand and smiled.

"It is sealed," he said. "The only way to open it is to poke a hole in the covering. You will be unable to puncture the covering, but a mythological being from my world can do it easily."

Harley returned the smile. "You knew that the crow was going to deliver the potion to Sammy...didn't you?"

"I am done here," Hephaestus said, brushing his meaty hands together.

"The rest is up to you two."

Harley lowered Hygea's cup into the pouch. He saw that the seal truly kept the liquid inside.

"It should make it all the way, TJ. Let's do this together."

He and TJ, two boys from JFK Middle School, who played soccer and lived in a cul-de-sac, closed the flap on the pouch and raised it to the sky.

Caw!

"It's all yours, Korvus," Harley called to their guide. "Take it to Sammy and save his life!"

The large black bird swooped down and hooked the strap of the heavy pouch in its claws. It circled several times before cawing a farewell. Harley and TJ watched until the messenger was a black speck on the horizon, then disappeared.

"Harley," TJ said. "Let's go home, now."

They looked around for a grove in which they could hide before performing their final disrobing and the linking amulet ritual—the one that would open the portal for home—and closed their eyes.

Somewhere a large dog barked eagerly. Azlynn and Tamiko each held up large towels around the circle. They, too, closed their eyes. The air changed—it rippled, causing them to hold their breath. The intensity of the air pressure pushed against them. Apollo barked wildly and began turning excited dog circles.

There was a popping sound, one that they hadn't heard when the boys left nearly three hours ago. Apollo was wagging his tail so hard that it nearly knocked Tamiko into the circle.

The towels were yanked from the girls' hands. Standing before them

were two smiling faces.

"We did it," Harley said. "We completed the quest."

"Let's go see Sammy," TJ laughed. "I got a feeling he's expecting us."

Somewhere in the distance a large black bird called to them, "Caw!"

EPILOGUE

Dr. Ammon allowed Harley and friends to enter Sammy's hospital room. Sammy had taken a turn for the worse, and Mrs. Crabtree wanted his friends to be able to say their good-byes so they could have some kind of closure.

"Mrs. Crabtree is quite distraught," the doctor told them. "It is she who has granted you permission to be in the room with Sammy."

The friends looked at each other, not understanding what was happening. Hadn't Harley and TJ completed the quest? They had all shared the same understanding that if nothing else, Sammy should at least wake up. Though not willing to say it out loud, each of them secretly worried that perhaps the whole thing had been a figment of their collective imagination. Maybe there was no portal to another time. Maybe there was no healing potion. Maybe their teacher had raised their hopes only to have them dashed to pieces at Sammy's bedside.

"Be very respectful, no matter how awful you feel," ordered Dr. Ammon.

The four friends tiptoed into the room. Mrs. Crabtree looked up and braved a smile. She opened her arms to them and hugged them generously.

"Thank you for being here," she told them. "You were the most important, wonderful friends my Sammy has ever known."

"Mrs. Crabtree," Tamiko said in especially soft tones, "Sammy is one our best friends."

"Yes," added Azlynn, "we want to be here for him and for you."

The five of them encircled Sammy's hospital bed. He lay in a deep sleep, yet a smile of sorts spread across his face. Wherever Sammy was, he seemed happy.

Nurse Fisher entered the room. She stood back, giving the group space to mourn the impending loss of a son and a friend. The machine monitoring Sammy's vitals began to slow its beeping. Beep…beep….beep…….beeeep.

Mrs. Crabtree leaned over her son. She had cried so much that it was difficult to realize that more tears could surface, but they did.

"Sammy," TJ started, "this is TJ. I'm sorry I didn't catch you before you hit the ground. I'm really sorry." Tears welled and he let them slide over his cheeks without shame.

"Sammy, this is Azlynn. I'm glad we shared the Harry Potter stories. I loved reading them to you."

Tamiko took a big breath. "Sammy, this is Tamiko. I really liked your stories and your poetry. When you come home, we'll have to write some more."

It was Harley's turn. "You know, Sammy, you told me to find the bird, and I did. You told me to hurry, and well…I really tried to get everything done as fast as I could. You can't go now. You have to fight to stay here with us and with your mom. She really needs you. So come home."

Sammy lay still. They looked at him through teardrops. Mrs. Crabtree leaned closer to kiss her son's forehead. "My baby, my son," she cried. "I love you so much. You are my heart and soul."

Harley could hardly watch. He did notice a tear fall from Mrs. Crabtree's eye onto Sammy's closed eyelid. In that very instant Sammy's foot twitched.

"Did you see that," Harley nearly yelled.

Nurse Fisher moved next to Harley in an effort to keep him from disrupting the solemnity of the moment.

"No, Nurse Fisher, his foot moved."

Sammy's other foot twitched. The nurse left the room to find the doctor. By the time they returned, Sammy was fully awake.

"It's a miracle," Mrs. Crabtree whispered through her tears.

Nurse Fisher moved to her side to keep her from collapsing to the floor. "Niobe," the nurse begged, "you must sit down."

TJ pulled the chair over to the women and Niobe Crabtree sat down. This time she was shedding tears of joy.

"You did it, Harley and TJ," Sammy said in a very hoarse voice. "You found him and he brought me the gift." Sammy seemed wide-awake and in full control of his cognition. "Thank you for not giving up."

"Sammy needs time to gain his strength," Dr. Ammon said. "You can come back tomorrow."

TJ got the doctor's attention. "He is going to be all right now." It wasn't a question; it was a statement. The universe felt right again.

Later that evening, Harley and TJ sat together in Harley's room. Both boys rubbed Apollo's sleek, golden coat. They shared so much without having to say a word.

"Harley," TJ said quietly.

"Yeah, TJ."

"Remember right before we left you were starting to tell me something, but you never finished."

"I remember."

"What was it?"

"Fourteen."

"What do you mean?"

"Did you know that Sammy's mother's name is Niobe?"

"I think I knew," TJ said, "so what?"

"I needed 14 teardrops—Niobe's tears," explained Harley. "I lost track and didn't know exactly how many had fallen into the bowl."

"Okay…"

"When Mrs. Crabtree's tear fell onto Sammy's eye, that was the 14th tear."

Sometime later, Sammy returned to school. He was always a happy kid, but now there was something even more sincere about him. He was stronger and much surer of himself.

Now, there were five of them and a dog: Harley, TJ, Tamiko, Azlynn, Sammy, and Apollo. This was their inner circle…this was true friendship.

www.ingramcontent.com/pod-product-compliance
Lightning Source LLC
LaVergne TN
LVHW011941070526
838202LV00054B/4748